The Journey into the Divided Hea
emptiness and brokenness of our day. Steve ...
one of our greatest needs, is anchored in relationships, both with God ...
foremost and with those we hold close. Get the relationship piece right and you
will be blessed; get it wrong and you will hurt.

- Dr. Tim Clinton
President of the American Association of Christian Counselors

The Journey into the Divided Heart creates a warm and thoughtful invitation into
life-changing relationship with God and people. We tend to want either private
healing with God or human connections with others. Steve Fair combines the
love of God and the love of people into one way of life and transformation.

- Rev. Jim Wilder, Ph.D.
Director of Life Model Works and author of *The Life Model: Living from the*
Heart Jesus Gave You

I believe that all of us have a divided heart to one degree or another. As
such, this book is not only for those who find themselves seeking healing for
emotional pain, but it is also for those reading this book cover and thinking
that they do not need it! Steve provides a lens for examining one's heart and
healing through an experiential and wonderful relational connection with God.
His book contains a very practical guide to exploring how we protect our own
hearts and thereby block our healing and a wholehearted love of God rather
than ultimately allowing God to be our protector. Steve then takes a fresh
look at biblical interventions and other suggestions that can be a huge help to
anyone on this journey.

- Rev. Canon Andrew Miller, LCSW
LCSW, Director of HeartSync Ministries

The Journey into the Divided Heart is a book which diagnoses "the signs
of the times," pinpointing in our current cultural climate the factors which
cause significant emotional and psychological distress. Steve Fair presents a
synthesis of the biological, psychological, and spiritual factors that underlie

much human suffering. It is balanced, insightful, and encouraging in an easily readable manner. Images and examples bring the underlying principles to life. In a seamless manner, this book explains the origins of defense mechanisms, the psychology behind them, and in particular the spiritual dimension. It portrays our need to invite the Healer into the broken areas of our lives and to allow ourselves to be vulnerable before God. It is hopeful in its presentation of many approaches to healing and freedom, which are based on God's healing presence, but does not neglect the biological and psychological. It can benefit any who read it with an open mind and trust in God's desire and ability to free us from the pains that bind us.

- Dr. Cheryl Mazzara, MD
Child and Adolescent Psychiatrist

What I remember most about being counseled by Steve Fair is his heart's desire to bring the session into the very throne room of God's presence. I have been counseled by others, but none brought that sense of intimacy. Steve certainly has a father's heart with a goal to bring someone into a deeper relationship with Abba Father God. How appropriate that he's titled his book *The Journey into the Divided Heart*. In every Christian there is tension between doing things their own way and God's way. This book, through the power of the Holy Spirit, will help reveal and bring healing to those places where the human heart is divided. The result can only be a greater intimacy with Abba Father. Those with a continued desire to know God better will be blessed by reading and applying the principles the author recommends.

- Dee Sochacki
Barnabas Ministries, Speaker, Author of *Amazing Grace: A Personal Testimony*

THE JOURNEY INTO THE
DIVIDED *Heart*

Helping You Face the Defense Mechanisms that Hinder True Emotional Healing

Steve Fair

5 Fold Media
Visit us at www.5foldmedia.com

Their heart is divided; now shall they be found faulty: he shall break down their altars, he shall spoil their images (Hosea 10:2 KJV).

Contents

Foreword

"The hardest road to walk is the one that leads inside yourself"
— Pastor Walt Caughel

As a minister and pastor most of my life I have not only witnessed how events and memory affect our lives, but I have lived it out myself. I came to my crisis of facing the question of who was I in my early college years. As depicted in the title of this book, *The Journey into the Divided Heart,* so was my heart divided. The stages of life, the wounds of childhood, the effects of growing up in mild poverty, confusion of religious life, and the pain of the world's systems came together, leaving me confused as to who I was. Emotions were filled with the joys and pains of my memories; friends seemed to come and go but none of them seemed to reach the depths of my heart anymore. Life was getting harder and my true person getting more lost in my everyday existence. It was during this time of my walk with God that He shared a very wise statement with me that would take most of the rest of my life to begin to understand. One day as I was struggling, He stated to me in prayer, "The hardest road to walk is the one that leads inside yourself." The rest of my life I would spend learning the depth of truth in that one sentence.

This book, *The Journey into the Divided Heart,* would have been a great tool in walking that road into this understanding. No matter what stage of life we are in, our hearts need to be healed. I would encourage anyone, no matter how they view themselves or their lives, to read this book. It gives insight into not only how we operate as humans in our thinking and defense mechanisms, but practical biblical steps to begin a new life today. A second benefit to gaining the truths revealed in these well-written pages is acquiring a better understanding of others. The benefits of understanding what a divided heart is and what can be done about it allow us to relate with others with more love and understanding. As we are less confused about our own memories and the effects they have, we will be more equipped to walk with those around us. What more wonderful tool to spread the love of God can there be than using our healed heart to walk with another on their road inside themselves?

Today I am as much walking this path as when I received this word. It has been a hard road taking an honest look inside my life at the guidance of the Holy Spirit. So many times the standards of the world around me or my own emotion would get in the way of seeing myself the way God sees me. Hurt, pain, and hope all mixed in a way that sometimes would make life hard to understand. Shame, fear, guilt, and anger would build walls that would direct these emotions at others or for me mostly aim them at myself. Maybe you can relate to having this same difficulty walking the road that leads inside of you?

I can tell you with confidence that though I am not finished with this road myself, it has been worth every challenge to stay on the path. In following the Holy Spirit inside myself, God has been able to reveal Himself to me in ways I would have never imagined when starting the journey. Areas that I thought would hurt forever have been healed, pain I was sure would never end He took away, and the love Jesus poured out inside my heart was amazing as it moved from being divided to whole, making the pain of life's reality not only bearable but overcomable.

From my own personal experience and that of all the people I have walked with over more than forty years in ministry I would offer this advice—don't quit!

When it hurts—press on.

When it seems hopeless—try again.

10

When you are sure you're right—accept that you might be wrong.

When you hate yourself—know Jesus loves you.

When you feel all alone—remember God never leaves us.

And above all else know that in Christ Jesus we have an eternity to live in Love.

This walk inside myself has made all the difference in my life and the lives of those I love. I encourage everyone who begins this road to the healing of a divided heart to keep their eyes on Jesus, the author and finisher of their faith, and to endure the pain of the challenge as unto our Savior Jesus Christ, enjoying each step of revelation and healing along the way as a true gift from God.

— Pastor Walt Caughel
Christians for a New Tomorrow Church

Introduction

One of the most graphic pictures painted for us in the whole Bible regarding relationship is that of the prophet Hosea being told by God to go marry a prostitute. God knew that she would leave him time and again and that Hosea would not only have to chase her down but would buy her back out of his own resources. This relationship was a symbolic picture of how we leave God and He continues to pursue us at great cost to Himself. Can you imagine being Hosea? This relationship between Hosea and his harlot wife, Gomer, was to be a sign and a symbolic picture to the people of Israel of who God is and who His people had become.

> *"When the Lord began to speak through Hosea, the Lord said to him, 'Go, take to yourself an adulterous wife and children of unfaithfulness, because the land is guilty of the vilest adultery in departing from the Lord.'" So he married Gomer daughter of Diblaim, and she conceived and bore him a son"* (Hosea 1:2-3).

God described His people and the state that they were in further in this book in the Bible, but He specifically says in Hosea 10:2 that they had "divided hearts."

> *"Their heart is divided"* (Hosea 10:2 KJV).

Their hearts were divided because, like Hosea's wife Gomer, they wanted God, but they also wanted their other lovers, which were the

13

other gods and idols of their day. They wanted to do things God's way, but they also wanted to do things their own way. They wanted God's love, protection, and provision, but they wanted to get these same things from other idols in their lives too. God called the division of their internal thinking a "divided heart," and He showed that their decisions and choices to do things their own way instead of God's had detrimental results in their lives. Their ways were unstable and inconsistent, and as we see in Gomer's life this ultimately led to emptiness, depression, and deep inner dissatisfaction. It's interesting to note that the consequences of their divided hearts are still the things so many struggle with today!

This divided heart problem is a big one, and we need some understanding of how the divided heart works if we are to live life to its fullest as Jesus instructed in John 10:10. My guess is that your heart, like mine and like those of the Israelites of that time, is divided too! God's goal is the same today as it was then. His aim was to pursue true love relationships with them by breaking off their unfaithfulness to other gods. They were being unfaithful to Him by "cheating" on Him just as Gomer cheated on Hosea. She rejected Hosea and ran to her other lovers, just as the Israelites turned their backs on God and ran to the altars and images of their other gods.

> *"Their heart is divided; now shall they be found **faulty**:*
> *he shall break down their altars, he shall spoil their*
> *images"* (Hosea 10:2 KJV).

God found them guilty of cheating on Him. He was confronting them and telling them that they were wrong. God disciplines those that He loves (Hebrews 12:6). He had been watching them and seeing the wrong path that they were headed down, and He was ready to intervene. Why did He choose to have Hosea go through all of this heartache? Why did He confront the Israelites and find fault with them? He was still in love with His people even after they went astray, and He wanted them to have a human example to illustrate that His heart felt the same way that ours does when it is betrayed.

Introduction

He was longing for His relationship with them to be restored, and He wanted His unfaithful wife back despite the fact that she (Israel) was breaking His heart! He is still longing for this today. He wants us to say, "I will come back to You, God." He knows that there is no true fulfillment in anything else that we have been chasing after other than Him.

> *"She will chase after her lovers but not catch them, she will look for them but not find them. Then she will say, 'I will go back to my husband as at first, for then I was better off than now'"* (Hosea 2:7).

With this prophetic backdrop, you are about to take a journey through the recesses of your own self to see where your heart is divided and what idols and altars you have built there. Rest assured, God's purpose was to bless His people in Hosea's time, and His purpose today is to bless and free you too. He just had to call them out of their double-minded, divided lives and into the life of freedom that He had created for them. He described how He wanted to bless them in Hosea 2:8-23 where He revealed His true heart, which was to provide everything they needed. Everything? He wanted to give them hope, real true love, compassion, protection from harm, safety, and security too. Read through those verses and you will see it is so.

My hope is that you will find all of these things and more as you read this book. This book is written for those who need and want true relief from the emotional pain that they carry (and this applies to all of us) and for those who work with those in pain. This book is for those who are pursuing their healing from the emotional damage of this world, especially those who have struggled with depression, anxiety, relational issues, anger, fear, trauma, and heartache. You may find out a lot about yourself as you read the following pages. You most likely will find out that you have false gods, idols, and altars in your life too, just as the Israelites did.

Our idols may not be actual little wooden carvings or altars where we give animal sacrifices as they did, but our idols may be no less powerful in our lives than these were to them. A god, or a "higher power" as secular rehab programs call it, is something we worship, something to which we submit and yield. A god or higher power is something we gain strength from, something we consult for answers, somewhere we look for protection, and someplace, which can be even inside of ourselves, where we find emotional and/or spiritual comfort and peace. Could it be that our culture has led us to a god and taught us a religion, a set of beliefs, and a means of doing life that relies on things that lead us off track—just as it did the Israelites in Hosea's time? Could this be a core reason why so many are anxious and depressed?

You will read about how today's idols are more centered around "self" than anything else. "Me" worship is the religion of our day, which is evident in our need for material possessions and constant entertainment, but even more so in the foundational mindsets of self-protection and self-preservation that make us think of ourselves instead of considering others relationally. It is interesting that this "me" worship and its accompanying stance of self-protection is recognized by both psychology and religion as being wholly unfulfilling to the human heart. Both groups know it is one of the root causes of depression and anxiety in our lives. Our self-centered mindsets are best seen in our emotional distancing—from one another and from God; they will be exposed and mapped out in our thinking and on a psychological level in this book. As God did to Israel with Hosea, we will also be confronted by what we read. Our spiritually divided hearts will be exposed as the cause behind our mental health and relational problems. We need new direction in life! We will discuss what a divided heart looks like and offer powerful interventions on how to bring change.

The Journey into the Divided Heart will take you through a beginning inventory of your heart, empowering you to take responsibility and either choose to be your own god, your own protector, and your own peace, or choose Someone bigger than yourself to be your leader. This is where our study of defense mechanisms comes to the fore. Though many of us have made idols out of things in our culture—like our jobs, our families, our money, our addictions, even our own self-image—all of us have idols in the form of our own set of defense mechanisms. We will review the psychology of defense mechanisms and share more about their purposes. They are just what they sound like—a defense. They are an internal psychological means of buffering us from feeling emotional pain. Thank God we have defense mechanisms; we need them. They are crucial to functioning successfully in our world. However, an overactive set of defense mechanisms may not just protect us from getting hurt or feeling anything negative; they may actually push us away from that which is healthy and good for us too. We feel protected and safe when we wall ourselves off from the world around us, and in many ways that is what most of us have been doing for years to keep ourselves above the flood waters of despair that this world often brings. Think about it. It was not many decades ago that three to four generations of family would live in the same house. It was not many decades ago that people stopped by each other's houses for a visit unannounced. It was not many decades ago that people lived life together as a community versus our present segregated and independent life of "us four and no more."

Where do we turn when we have problems? What do we do when we have pain and heartache? Where do we seek comfort, security, and peace when life does not go the way we think it should? The human heart has many directions it takes in times of hardship—it runs towards that which brings instant relief, and it often runs away from that which it needs. Its wants and its needs many time contradict themselves and leave it always wanting. What we want emotionally is to feel no pain and be at ease all the time. However, the "dis-ease" of today is greater than ever before because our defenses, trained in denial, have taught us to pursue a lifestyle and a state of being that God wanted for us at the beginning of creation but has long since been lost.

The Journey into the Divided Heart

It is time we saw how our hearts are divided because without an understanding of this we will continue in ignorance, repeating the patterns of our past over and over again. God created our hearts, so much of our discussion about our hearts and the healing of our hearts must focus us on Him and on spiritual issues. Christian and non-Christian readers alike, please stick with these pages! Deny the attempts of your defense mechanisms to cover what the Bible describes as the *"deep waters"* of your heart (Proverbs 20:5) and shield you from the tough spiritual questions that need to be explored and resolved in you so that you can find the truly fulfilling life that you were created to have.

Chapter 1: The State of Our Hearts

Some of us have embraced the medical model almost exclusively, which says that the symptoms and problems we have are rooted only in a medical and physical origin, and so the solutions to their problems are found exclusively in medical interventions. However, some of us are learning to look for the origins of our problems and symptoms in our emotions, and believing the solutions to our problems with anxiety and depression are found in talking about our feelings alone. The missing link is found in understanding that there are spiritual origins to the problems of our hearts too, and if we put the physical, the emotional, and the spiritual together, we will find not only ways to cope but ways to actually heal! Get ready to heal if you can focus on all three parts of who we are—body, soul, and spirit. We will see, though, that the majority of our attention needs to be on the spiritual end because it has been so neglected and misunderstood. As I begin to describe the heart and the process of healing from a spiritual perspective, I will cite multiple Scripture verses with their references so you can look them up and find out what God has to say directly. God definitely makes the best counselor!

As we begin to understand the ways that our hearts are divided and the ways that our hearts protect themselves from emotional pain, I am confident that we can learn to better love ourselves, love others, and to love the Lord our God with *all* our heart (see Deuteronomy 6:5). Life is all about *love,* isn't it? Happiness and fulfillment are also all about *love* too, aren't they? Yet to give and receive true love we need to grab hold of the revelation that our hearts are truly broken into pieces and unable to give and receive true love in the way in which they were created. Though we are longing for true loving relationship, our hearts are divided in that we are resisting true loving relationships with others and with God both at the same time!

THE UNFAITHFUL HEART

We do not have to live as a "Gomer" but can live life with a faithful heart and the actions that go with it. We will explore seventeen different defense mechanisms we use to protect our hearts from emotional pain, and we will also specifically cover dissociation, a defense that we all use at different levels of intensity, but one most of us are completely unaware of. When we look at our desires, thoughts, and emotions, it's clear that our hearts are divided. This is especially true when some of these defense mechanisms are operating without us even knowing they exist! Dissociation is a great example of this.

In school preparing for social work back in the early 1990s, we were taught that you might see one to two dissociative cases in your whole career. We were taught that dissociation disorders were a rare and controversial phenomenon that were most often connected with what was then called multiple personality disorder. However, we are finding that this is not the case, and this splitting of our consciousness into "alters" is not as uncommon as we previously thought. The Scripture even shows one of the main purposes for Christ's coming to earth is His *binding up the brokenhearted* (see Isaiah 61:1 KJV), which actually means He came to bind up the fragmented heart. Jesus came to help the dissociated heart!

Some estimate that diagnosable dissociative disorders are represented in fourteen percent of the general public, putting the numbers of people suffering from this disorder at a staggering thirty million people. Other professionals estimate that one percent of our general population, or well over two million people in America have a diagnosable dissociative identity disorder (DID). This does not even include those who have

20

symptoms of dissociation insufficient to diagnose. In our counseling centers and churches, we are seeing dissociation not as a rare disorder but as a prevalent primary defense mechanism employed by everyone who has experienced trauma of any level early in life. Professionals in ministry and psychology are finding that dissociation is not only very common but present in the majority, not the minority. It is a simple defense mechanism manifesting anywhere from very subtle base levels of intensity to full blown split personalities that retain the traumatic emotions of the past.

Many of our defense mechanisms are primitive, subtle, and automatically used as a reflex to prevent us from feeling even low level traumas from early on in life. Truly, dissociation is one of the first-line defenses that our minds and hearts use to handle trauma, abandonment, rejection, hurt, and fear. We will study this further, along with many other defense mechanisms that are much more subtle and difficult to discern. Out of His great mercy, God hardwired these defenses into us to be used during times of emotional trauma and hardship in the same way that He gave our physical bodies the ability to go into shock when a level of physical pain is more than we can bear. Persons who have used dissociation and other defense mechanisms as children often continue to use them subconsciously to protect themselves emotionally from any ongoing triggers that they think will bring renewed emotional hurt and pain. Though these defenses are God-given and hardwired in us, by continuing to use them later in life to block and cope with pain from the past and present we are unconsciously taking control of the protection of our own hearts, even while confessing that we have given all control at salvation to our Lord Jesus! When we are unaware of our defense mechanisms, our hearts are hidden, even from ourselves. We make choices to protect ourselves, sometimes in ways that are highly destructive. This ongoing and often unconscious state of living is the primary cause of many of our present-day issues. We are hurting ourselves daily while somewhere deep inside we are believing that our past is the cause of our difficulties. If we can embrace the fact that the ways we are psychologically defending ourselves may be more of the problem than the actual origins of the problems we have, then we will be able to take significant steps toward a life of freedom, fulfillment, and healing.

The Journey into the Divided Heart

As an example, defenses such as dissociation, like castle walls, keep our foes and their emotional triggers at bay, but they also serve to keep friends and loved ones from entering our hearts. Acting in this self-protective manner, we are often subconsciously distancing ourselves not only from others but from our God as well. The way we protect ourselves becomes the actual cause of our isolation; loneliness and the resulting depression symptoms soon follow. As God said in Genesis, *"It is not good for the man to be alone"* (Genesis 2:18). When our defenses lead us to isolate ourselves, we, like Adam, will be left in a state of emptiness even if we have everything we want in life just as Adam had in his garden paradise. One of the goals of this book is to equip people to have spiritual discernment to detect their defense mechanisms and defend themselves against the way those mechanisms steal life's blessings instead. Once we can recognize our defenses, then we can choose to drop our subtle guards and replace them. My hope is that you will replace your reliance on them with a reliance on the One who is the true protector of our hearts! Only then may we experience the full love, joy, peace, and patience that we desire (Galatians 5:22).

Many of us are unaware that we are living in a brokenhearted state! Our hearts have been traumatized, but we have a narrow definition of trauma that hinders us from ever considering that our hearts have been broken. You will see as you read further that just because you don't feel that your heart is broken doesn't mean that it isn't. You will see how dissociation is really a fragmenting or a splitting of our free will inside, and an unplugging from our own emotions and even some of our memories that began early in life. Early on, many people learned to hide their pain, pretending that everything was fine emotionally. They learned to disconnect from their own hearts and emotions.

WHY ARE YOU HIDING?

As people go through this process of recognizing their defenses and exposing their hearts, they also see that they can attach, relate, and love like never before! In a place of complete vulnerability, our hearts can operate in true intimacy just like Adam and Eve did in the garden. They walked personally with their God in the cool of the day (Genesis 3:8).

The State of Our Hearts

It's our shame and the various traumas (both abuses and neglects) that we have been through that have led us to hide from each other and from God, making relationship and intimacy nearly impossible.

In Genesis 3, God questioned Adam and Eve, saying *"Where are you?"* as they were hiding from God after they broke the one rule He gave them: Don't eat the forbidden fruit.

> *"But the Lord God called to the man, 'Where are you?'*
> *He answered, 'I heard you in the garden, and I was afraid*
> *because I was naked; so I hid.' And he said, 'Who told you*
> *that you were naked? Have you eaten from the tree that I*
> *commanded you not to eat from?'"* (Genesis 3:9-11).

God was not asking where they were for His own information; He already knew (Matthew 10:26-30). God asked this question to Adam then and to all of us today to prompt us to look within ourselves. He wants to expose us to ourselves! Shame led Adam and Eve to hide. Their hearts were divided—they wanted to follow God's ways, but they had also decided to follow the temptations of the serpent that had led them to this act of rebellion.

The result of this? They naturally and automatically began to hide! They avoided God's presence and sought distance between them and Him. They sewed fig leaves together to physically hide their bodies, their nakedness, which they were not even aware of before this time. It didn't bother them that they were naked and vulnerable *before* they ate the forbidden fruit, but after they disobeyed, nothing else was more important to them than to cover themselves and distance themselves from God. Could this be part of what is happening in your life and in your heart today? It may be that your divided heart has followed your own ways and that you are hiding because you know these ways are not working. This is the same natural and almost unconscious reaction of self-protection that Adam and Eve had!

Maybe you are blaming yourself for some things that were not at all your fault too. You may think God is mad at you, or you may just be mad at yourself. You may be one of those perfectionist personalities who has a lot of negative thoughts about yourself. Or you may have made some bad decisions and you don't know the difference between conviction, which leads to making better life decisions, and condemnation, which leads to shame-based feelings about yourself. Whatever it is, many of us are hiding, and we may not even know why! You are hiding as Adam and Eve did, covering yourself as they did, but not necessarily with fig leaves. Maybe that too, who knows? You are hiding yourself with your defense mechanisms, your walls, your idols, your addictions. God's purpose in exposing you is to free you; the price for your sin was already paid. There is great relief in exposure, great relief in coming into the light and being honest with yourself and others, without shame. It's time to remove the fig leaves and return to the state of naked vulnerability that you were created to walk in. You may be convicted right now—convicted about some things you are hiding—and if you can stay out of condemnation, there may be thoughts in you right now that would lead you to telling others what you are going through. That's a healthy first step to coming out of hiding. If so, take a moment to ponder these thoughts, and don't let your divided heart lead you back into hiding but rather into some first steps of vulnerability. Ask yourself, what am I hiding inside? What would happen if I stopped hiding my sins, my feelings, my thoughts or my memories?

In order to grow, we need to take responsibility, not only for the behavioral decisions that we make but also for our motives, the reasons we do what we do. For the Christian who has read the Word at all, we know that from God's perspective it is our responsibility to bring all things into the light (John 3:21), to expose our hearts (1 Corinthians 4:5), to be led into all truth by the Holy Spirit (John 16:13), to take every thought captive (2 Corinthians 10:5), to exercise good discernment about all things (John 7:24), to be like Jesus and do only what the Father has us do (John 5:19), and to let Christ live through us by being crucified to ourselves daily (Galatians 2:20). At times, this feels like an impossible lifestyle to pursue, but God will accomplish this in us if we will cooperate with Him!

> *"For it is God who works in you to will and to act according to his good purpose"* (Philippians 2:13).

The State of Our Hearts

Acts that lead to sanctification are our mandate and our responsibility, but they are truly not possible unless our divided hearts turn wholly to Him. We have to humble ourselves in the sight of our Lord first (James 4:10) and then we seek Him with all of our hearts (Matthew 6:33). We are told to study to show ourselves approved unto men (2 Timothy 2:15), and by becoming sensitive to the prompting of the Holy Spirit, He will guide us out of the state of self-protection and the defenses that we rely too heavily on and into a state of trusting Him (John 7:39). This process can all begin when we decide to come out of hiding.

How can we hear Him, the One who dwells in our hearts, when we are walled off and dissociated even from ourselves? It's much easier to receive conviction from the Holy Spirit about a divided heart if we are able to see the level of self-protection that we use daily to control our own lives. Are you ready to hear Him convict you and show you your defenses? If your answer is yes, then God is already working in your life because your heart has been humbled, softened, and is eager to grow. If you cannot answer yes, don't despair. You just have a well-defended, divided heart that God is ready to work on and heal when and only if you give Him permission. You can start this "journey inside yourself" as you read about in the foreword by simply praying, "God, I give You permission to work on and heal my divided heart."

We keep coming back to this issue of responsibility. As you allow God to soften your heart, remember it is our glory, our ability, and our responsibility to search out our hearts.

> *"It is the glory of God to conceal a matter; to search out a matter is the glory of kings"* (Proverbs 25:2).

The heart and its defenses are our responsibility and our glory to search out, but the cost of searching inside of ourselves is that we will see all that God wants to show us. It's scary to think about what we may find inside. Maybe there are some hard memories that will surface—our hurt, fear, wounds, traumas, confusion, anger, and any other unsettled issues we harbor deep inside of us. The glory of the matter, though, is that we also get to find the hidden treasures and the true Godlikeness of our own hearts. Remember, He created us in His image (Genesis 1:27).

What an exciting time to walk the face of this earth. As the Word of God describes it, we are living in a period of time that is close to His second coming. We are living in a time when He says that He is coming back for a bride (the church—we His people) without *"spot or wrinkle"* (Ephesians 5:27 NKJV). The Lord also says that judgment starts in the house of the Lord (1 Peter 4:17). Before He comes to clean the world up, He has said that He will come and clean us up by judging and revealing to us the true motives of our hearts. Instead of our emotions holding us hostage and causing us to dissociate because of them, it's time that we learn to regulate our emotions and take the thoughts behind them captive to follow Christ. It is time for our emotional freedom to come to the fore. It's time for us to walk in the love, peace, and joy promised to us as part of living life to its fullest (Galatians 5:22; John 10:10).

Let's take this journey of a thousand miles by starting with a single step, by first gaining an overall perspective of the calling of the Lord toward the healing of our hearts and then by studying the defenses we use to protect ourselves emotionally. We will lay a foundation for our understanding of these defenses before discussing the interventions that God is giving us to tear these walls down. Follow along prayerfully and with hope for personal emotional, physical, and spiritual healing. I pray that it will manifest without hindrance in you as your divided heart is healed. As you read, if you hear the voice of the Lord, *"do not harden your hearts"* as the Bible says in Psalms 95:8, but let these pages lead you to a place of softening and brokenness from which you will be able to receive the blessings that God has for you. No striving or psychoanalyzing is needed. You only need a decision of your will to remove and replace every defense that is hiding your heart!

Chapter 2: The Heart Divided from Hope

"Hope deferred makes the heart sick, but a longing fulfilled is a tree of life" (Proverbs 13:12).

Let's settle for nothing less than the best God has for us! The hearts that are choosing to defer or write off their hopes are likely very well-defended hearts that have actually been hurt and are using hopelessness as a defense mechanism (read more about this in the defense mechanism section). God has given us as His children open access to communicate with Him and be connected with Him at all times. He has given us the capacity for giving and receiving true, unconditional love from Him and from others that results in an intimacy and unity with Him and other people on a level that we think is reserved only for spouses and close family members. God has provision of health and finances for you, and He even has plans for communities without hatred, violence, or ethnic disunity.

In what areas of your life have you been settling for less, deferring and giving up hope? Where has your hope been deferred, leaving your heart sick, as it says above? What areas of your life on earth do not match up to all that you will have in heaven? These are the places where this book will challenge you to begin hoping!

The Journey into the Divided Heart

Take a moment and write down below three areas in which you feel hopeless.

1. _____

2. _____

3. _____

YOUR HOPING HISTORY

Let's focus on the heart divided from relational hope. Take a moment and consider those you have respected the most in your life, those who have been loving and wholesome models to you. You loved them with an unfailing love! More than just good people, these were your personal heroes and saints you have at one point or another in your life put on a pedestal. Maybe it was a sweet grandparent who always gave you the benefit of the doubt. Maybe it was a teacher who always looked you in the eye with hope and acceptance. Maybe it was a best friend you skipped down the road with, hand in hand, with no thoughts of what the world might think. Maybe these people were even pastors or kind-hearted Sunday school teachers who talked about their love for others and for Jesus.

Do you remember how you treasured every word these people said to you, longing to hear more from them, as it seemed as though they regarded you as the most important person in the whole world? Do you remember how fulfilled and safe you felt as you just enjoyed time together and laughed and played? Security, safety, and satisfaction were the fruit of having relationship with those you looked up to so highly. Sadly, some of you have not had even one person in your life you can use for this example. If this is you then your heart was and is truly traumatized. We will address this in the intervention section later. Through the lack and neglect of having such an example of true relationship, you missed out on a precious need of your heart—to love and be loved! It's from these relationships that we learn to operate *in hope* that there may be, and could be, a possibility that there is a human being or two on the earth who is special to us, to whom we are special, and who we can *fully trust*!

To those who do have examples of people you have truly admired and trusted, you know that your heart did something interesting around these types of people. Your heart felt safe, and it decided to fully engage. In that place of trust, your heart lowered its guard, took off its fig leaves, and let itself be drawn into a place of closeness with others. In this vulnerable state, whether with a parent, a friend, a lover, a pastor, a mentor, or whomever, you took a risk and did what hearts do without defense mechanisms—you became like what the Bible describes as a little child (Luke 18:16), and you were content to be fully vulnerable, fully *you*!

Do you remember that place of being fully *you*—the state of having no guardedness and no protective measures in place to hide your true self? It is a pretty incredible place to be! If you do remember, then you will also recall that you didn't have that skeptical look in the corner of your eye and you weren't worried about what the other person might say or do. You didn't have any questioning in your heart about whether they were right or wrong all the time when they spoke to you. You didn't have rebuttals, and you didn't need to think of what you wanted to say back when you were listening to them. You weren't afraid of being hurt, used, or judged. You didn't have to protect yourself at all! Your guard was so far down that you didn't fear closeness, nor did you have the normal personal space issues that usually distanced you from others. You just wanted to sit in Grandma's lap and be listened to. You just wanted to be held in the arms of that special person in your life because it was safe in their arms! You just wanted to see their face light up as they said, "Hello!" It showed you that you were important! God built you to need this.

This place of defenselessness has no worry, no twitching or tension, no butterflies in your stomach, and a complete peace even when there are no words being said between the two of you. No words are needed because acceptance fills any empty spaces in your heart like a safety net, allowing you to feel the connections between yourself and others whether you are together or apart. There is no being offended in this place of vulnerability. There's no distancing. No preferring to be anywhere else. There is an attachment that comes from a defenseless trust that can happen almost instantly and does not depend on time together. In that place, you truly are like a little child. You are behaving like a "sheep," as the Bible compares us to in John chapter 10, as a defenseless lamb. Though a great many have not enjoyed this in even one relationship, an experience like this can feed hope and cause you to take risks to get that kind of intimacy and relationship even more. It is only in this state of defenselessness of heart that our need for love and relationship can truly be met. It is only in this place that we can attach to ourselves, others, and God. It is only in this place that we are not alone.

THE "CRASH AND BURNS" OF THE HOPEFUL HEART

What often happens with these types of attachments is that pain follows love, because there is eventually some sort of hurt or let down in that relationship. There comes an act of betrayal and rejection (purposeful or not), abuse and neglect, or there is a hope deferred that makes your heart sick (Proverbs 13:12). Maybe loved ones didn't want to spend as much time with you as you would have liked. Maybe you felt replaced by someone else and that broke your heart. Maybe the hurt was much more pronounced in that there was trauma through sexual, physical, or emotional abuse that came from a person who was supposed to be your protection. Maybe they spoke words behind your back, gossiped, or slandered you, leaving you feeling unloved. Maybe there was no real hurt at all, but rather a mispercieved and misinterpreted let down that stung as if it were real.

Our unconscious hope is often that our "favorite people" will meet all our needs—that they will carry us whenever we fall and be the safety that our hearts have longed for. Because we put so many of our eggs in these relational baskets, we experience not only love but great pain and disappointment too. People will always disappoint us because they are human, just like us. Unfortunately, the pedestal that they live on in our minds comes crashing down, leaving us hurt and wounded. We crash and burn and quickly learn that we don't want that to happen again. It's then that our defenses internally come to life and offer solutions and protection against the pain that we feel in our hearts. Like implanted viruses in our minds, our defenses begin to tell us how to run away, hide, retaliate, and seek cover automatically. Our hearts feel such pain when we are hurt by those with whom we were vulnerable that we not only run away from them and seek cover from that person specifically, but we determine to run away and seek cover from anyone who may get that close to us again or anyone similar to the one who hurt us. We find ourselves fleeing relationships in general. Where we were previously pursuing, we find ways to justify and explain to ourselves the reasons that we should isolate ourselves instead. "Once bitten, twice shy," right? We are well practiced at this art of defending ourselves by adulthood, because our hearts as kids hoped for the innocent relationships that God wanted for us, but they got burned instead. We call this process "growing up."

How fast the skill of defending ourselves is developed, and how small the triggers really need to be to get us in such a stance. It may be as simple as a phone call that was not returned, and it may be as normal as that favorite someone having a bad day that we then take personally. We tell our hearts to protect themselves. "Shields up, red alert!" Friends become foes, and our hearts treat others as if they were our enemies by protecting and hiding our true feelings from them. We start young and develop these defenses over time. But the results are dreadful—our relationships stay shallow and we miss out on blessings galore! The once soft heart that was uninhibited and free got burned, developed its own ways to protect itself from getting hurt again, and grew up, leaving that innocent and hopeful heart behind.

THE BROKEN SPIRIT

The Bible talks about a "broken spirit" as the fruit of being deeply hurt, or even the perception of being hurt. We often feel quite literally broken—deep down inside. We loved, and then we lost! We trusted, and we felt betrayed! We hoped and we were sorely disappointed! We are given insight over a dozen times in the Old Testament about the brokenhearted or those with a broken spirit, and I believe this is how many of us are. Our spirits are broken early in life before we even have a chance to experience our true identity.

The word *broken* is a descriptor that deserves some attention, and when referencing the human heart this word clearly describes the ability of our innermost self to be injured, destroyed, crushed, split into pieces, and then separated from itself. The broken spirit is no different from a broken piece of pottery. A broken piece of pottery has gone through some type of trauma. Something was aimed at it, or it took some fall so steep that it cracked and shattered. Likewise, a broken heart withstood (through no fault of its own) a circumstance that led to its demise. Something happened to it that so greatly disturbed it that its internal glue was compromised, and the pottery fell apart, sometimes into dozens of pieces. From what the Word of God describes, your spirit and your heart could literally be broken!

What does a broken spirit look like according to Scripture? Scripture indicates that a broken spirit has *"bitter grief"* (Ezekiel 21:6) and that no one can bear it (Proverbs 18:14). It tells us that crying and wailing are symptoms of a broken spirit (Isaiah 65:14) and that a broken spirit *"dries up the bones"* (Proverbs 17:22). We also learn that the broken spirit comes from scorn (Psalms 69:20) and from a deep *"sorrow of the heart"* (Proverbs 15:13 NKJV). Thoughts of death and feelings of having no security follow close to a broken spirit. The broken spirit has no joy, loses its sense of self, and *"dwells on the insults and hostilities that it has endured"* (Job 17:1-2). Scripture has much to say about this condition. Becoming aware of some of these symptoms and how common they can be in our cruel world makes one wonder if any of us has escaped having at least a fractured, if not broken, spirit.

When we do suffer a fractured or a broken spirit, there is oftentimes an "arrested development" at the time that the spirit is broken, leaving it to operate and perceive the world at that particular age and developmental stage of life. The verbal curses against one's self-worth are imprinted permanently on the broken pieces of the heart until healing is received.

"You'll never amount to anything," "You are bad," and "It is all your fault," whether spoken or just perceived, become basic beliefs and fragments of the broken heart that are stored and replayed in the mind whenever they are triggered. Once we believe these kinds of lies, it is hard to believe anything different, and we stay stuck in that negative definition of ourselves long term. The broken pieces of our heart can't heal while they are still stuck in the past.

As was the case with Job, his broken spirit even cried out for death, as he said *"the grave awaits me"* and *"my days are cut short"* (Job 17:1). There is a separation from life inside of a person, and a spirit of death can overcome a person with thoughts of suicide or, even more subtly, a general sense of hopelessness and helplessness that things will never get better. These symptoms describe clinical depression and what God calls a *"spirit of heaviness"* (Isaiah 61:3 NKJV), which often comes with a broken spirit.

Has your heart or spirit been broken? Maybe you have felt that spirit of heaviness and depression. If you have, has it ever felt like things are simply hopeless? Has the heaviness ever gotten to the point where you even thought of taking your life? Even these thoughts are defense mechanisms that we will talk about soon. They are all symptoms manifesting from a heart that is ready for some healing. Healing is available, and relief is around the corner. We can pray that your broken heart be healed and put back together and that you can see the original plan of who God truly made you to be. We can pray that your true identity and purpose can then be revealed more clearly as you see the broken pieces of your spirit come back together into their original and amazing form.

THE EYES TELL IT ALL

I am a big believer in the concept of the eyes being the window of the soul. When a person has a broken spirit or a splitting of the spirit, there is a distinct look that I have often seen in the eyes of those who have suffered such pain. You might have seen that broken-spirited look in the faces of refugees in the news who just came out of traumatic situations. They have what I call "the deer-in-the-headlights look"—hollow and empty, confused and disoriented. But they also have that frozen, trapped stare that lets you know that they are in a mode of survival and shock because of the trauma they have endured. This state of broken-spiritedness always has strong defenses that develop with it to help us feel we are surviving. This state of brokenness nearly always involves dissociation on some level in the individual too.

You may have this same look and are just unaware of it, or you cover it well with some of your defenses. Others might be able to tell you that you have this look, and if not, you can check by looking into your own eyes. That's right! You can look into your own eyes—it's really not as hard as you might think. Have you ever looked deep into your own eyes? Most of us have never really tried. It seems like an odd thing to do. I remember the first time the Lord led me to take a deep, deep look into my own eyes. It can be a most enlightening, yet scary, experience. It is difficult for most of us to look at ourselves in the mirror at all because of the self-hatred (complete lack of love for self) we have, especially physically. We immediately notice all that we do not love about our bodies and pull away from looking at the creation that God has made us to be. How sad that is! But if you can get past the physical, you may be able to focus on what your eyes are telling you about what is in your soul, and you may notice a real "lost" look in your eyes hidden deeply beneath the surface. You might see lots of pain too. Take a moment and give this a try. Look at yourself in the mirror, focus especially on your eyes and write down here what you see (with your defenses down):

_____

_____

_____

_____

_____

_____

The Heart Divided from Hope

This lost look and all the other pain inside can be masked and hidden by our behaviors, our hyperactivity, our sense of humor, our avoidance, and any other defense mechanisms we have developed. The eyes tell the story, though, if you look past all of the externals and let yourself see the pain, the heaviness, the confusion, the anger, the fear, the rage, and the despair that still exists as a scar on the hearts of even those of us who seem to be the most "well put together." Underneath all this pain you will find buried treasure. You may have seen a broken heart, a broken spirit, and though this is painful and shocking to realize, it may allow you to see the places inside of you that the Lord desires so wholeheartedly to *heal!* You may also see beauty in your eyes that you have not noticed ever before. You will see so much in yourself and in the eyes of others too if you choose to let yourself.

THE PROGRESSION OF BROKENNESS

A person's spirit can become fragmented and broken, just like our nursery rhyme "Humpty Dumpty" says when we "have a great fall." God's horsemen and God's men try to put Humpty together again, but many times the wounded heart, once bitten, becomes "twice shy." Imagine then what the damage of ongoing and consistent wounds to a vulnerable heart can produce. Oftentimes, the pain of these wounds is stored somewhere deep inside the soul and spirit where it is protected even from our own memory and consciousness (dissociation). This pain may manifest when triggered at times by similar experiences in life. It may manifest in physical symptoms (especially anxiety, fear-based tension, and pain). It especially manifests in a person living in a vacuum of intimate relationships. No longer does this heart that once trusted allow love to flow freely; instead, it grows calloused, transforming from the childlike nature it was created to thrive in to a self-protecting and pious adult condition that is often anxious and controlled. This becomes the person's new normal. They live life in the relational shallow end instead of jumping into the deep end of the pool. The shallow end doesn't have a lot of pain because it doesn't have a lot of triggers and the person's wounded, lonely, and brokenhearted state is not even noticeable to them. Only circumstances that trigger them can bring pain temporarily to the surface. "I'm fine," they will answer. "It's all good!" Even so, others see their divided heart as well as the heavy load they carry deep inside.

Think of the dangers of a deceived and defensive heart using this football illustration: What if you were on a football team, and all the coach ever sent out was the defense? What would happen to your team if the defense was sent out, not only to stop the other team's offense but for all the special teams and offensive plays as well? What if the defense was always on duty? Bear with me, non-sports fans! When questioned, what if the coach said that his reasoning was, "At any point the opposing team might try to score and this could hurt our chances of winning"? That coach would be fired at once because, first of all, he would never win a game. But most of all, he has lost sight of what football is really about. It is about taking ground, scoring points, and winning the game. We too are in a contest, and the Bible says that we are to run the race for the prize that is set before us (1 Corinthians 9:24), and anything less than moving forward wholeheartedly leaves us in the position of losing out on life. The divided, broken heart doesn't take ground though; they maintain where they are, living safely within their defense mechanisms and comfort zones. The progression of brokenness leads to complacency, and we as a team in our communities, in the church, and in the world, lose the game!

We lose because we live life in a defensive stance, our hearts divided from the hope He has placed within us. Take a minute and ask God to restore your hope, to give you a heart "undivided," and to proceed through this book with the expectation that you will conquer all that is hindering you.

"I will give them an undivided heart and put a new spirit in them" (Ezekiel 11:19).

Chapter 3: Counting the Cost of Healing

The divided heart is a heart in denial, filled with ignorance and defensive against the truth of God. The Lord wants to fully occupy our hearts, but being told that one has these defenses will often lead the defended heart to automatically impede itself (on some level) from even considering that it needs help. The dissociated and defended heart tends to miss conviction and defend itself against all heart exposure, even that based in love. The dissociated and defended heart is unable, and unconsciously unwilling, to look at the depth to which it is still in control of itself as it numbly avoids the conviction of the Holy Spirit who lovingly says to us that *"you are wretched, pitiful, poor, blind"* before telling us that He has so much more for us if we would only be humble enough to trade in our ways for His (Revelation 3:17).

The Bible says to "count the cost" before you build, for it would be unwise to start something and not be able to finish (Luke 14:28). The main "cost" to healing your heart is not necessarily physical, but emotional. The pursuit of having a healed and whole heart is to feel the weight of the darkness still there and to take responsibility for it.

Have you ever seen the true dichotomy of your own heart? Have you ever watched yourself bless others and with the same mouth then judge and accuse? How is it that a place as beautiful as our hearts can be occupied by both light and darkness, love and anger, even hate and good will at the same time? How is it that out of a good heart can flow such

The Journey into the Divided Heart

strong words of love and light, while cursing and chaos are spoken by this same tongue? First John 2:9 tells us what is happening when we see both the light and darkness existing simultaneously within ourselves. It says, *"He that saith he is in the light, and hateth his brother, is in darkness"* (1 John 2:9 KJV).

John is saying that when we see hate in our hearts, we are deceived if we think we are "walking in the light." We think we are walking in the light and we say that we are Christians, but the words that come from our hearts expose the true condition that our hearts are in—they are filled with darkness that needs our attention! It is our hearts' holy desires that enable us to walk in the light on all occasions, with no darkness hidden inside. It is only with an understanding of the divided heart that we are able to grasp how hope and hate can operate inside of us simultaneously. We can begin to live from a place of true hope by simply inviting the light to come into every room of our hearts that may still be harboring hidden darkness. The cost of this process can be excruciating at times because of all that has been "swept under the rug" and that is yet to be grieved and healed, but the end is worth the trouble.

In counting the cost of our healing, we must first look at the hopes and dreams for relationship that were built into us by God who knew that *"it is not good for the man to be alone"* (Genesis 2:18). The cost of realizing and feeling this lack of relationship that we once allowed ourselves to hope and yearn for brings with it deep feelings of emptiness and pain. The greatest cost of our healing is usually in facing the history of our hearts having been broken as a result of being betrayed in our past.

Though there are obstacles and costs to our healing and it is scary to proceed, there are great benefits to be realized. The cost of healing comes mostly in challenging emotions we must engage as we peel back the calluses, pull off the scabs, and remove bandages from the aged places of pain, unforgiveness, and hurt in our hearts. The goal of revisiting those painful places from the past is twofold. We learn to recognize the defenses that we developed at that time, and we bring peaceful closure to the emotional traumas themselves! We don't need fifteen years of deep psychotherapy to analyze all that happened in our past, but *we do need to feel in order to heal,* and we need to map out our defenses well enough so we are able to recognize them when they try to rise up in the future. Healing, then, is a state of being whole, and this wholeness is found through living life outside of your defenses.

A friend who took this journey inside her heart saw what she described to be "a huge river behind a dam that held back the tears, the anger, and the pain" of her past. Later she had a vision in which she was plugging holes in the dam with her every finger and toe to hold back what was pressuring against the dam. The dam symbolized her walls and defenses. She counted the cost of pulling her fingers from the holes in the dam and watching the wall release all that was held behind it. She said "yes" to the Spirit of God calling her toward healing and bravely reconnected with her own heart's emotions. She wrote me this letter to share with my clients to encourage those who would be starting their healing process. Later in the letter, she uses an illustration from C.S. Lewis, which describes this same healing process.

Hello friend,

If you are reading this letter, it means that you are also sitting in the chair next to Steve's desk. I encourage you to take the journey that lies before you. There will be times when you think the pain and tears will never stop—but hang in there—they will! I cannot tell you how many hours I cried, how physically sick I felt, how emotionally torn, bruised, and beaten I felt. There were many times when I wished that I had never even started the process of exposing the dark places in my heart.

Don't be surprised if you leave sessions angry with God, Steve, and basically most of your world. I left Steve's office more than once very upset with God and Steve, and sometimes just with Steve. Those were the times when Steve was leading me out of my comfort zone and into some scary territory. "This isn't fair!" was the cry of my heart. "Why do I have to be the one to go through all of this pain when it seems like no one else is being held accountable—just me?"

The Journey into the Divided Heart

You can let your guard down and express and feel what is in your heart. It does not matter if what you are feeling and expressing is ugly. Even when I left a session upset with Steve and the whole counseling process, I could rest assured that when I walked into my next counseling session Steve would be there with an open mind, heart, and arms with a hug, waiting.

No one else can take your place and do what needs to be done. This is a journey that only you can take. Your journey will not be exactly like my journey, but the underlying need will always be the same. Our central need is God, His Son, and His Holy Spirit. There is no other way to complete healing.

Years ago, I read *The Chronicles of Narnia* by C.S. Lewis. In the fifth book of that series, *The Voyage of the Dawn Treader,* we meet the children's cousin, Eustace. Eustace finds himself in terrible circumstances because of the choices that he has made in his life. He discovers that he has turned into a dragon. Eustace finally meets Aslan the great lion (Jesus). Aslan tells Eustace to undress himself—take off the dragon skin and enter the pool of healing. Eustace starts scratching himself and the scales and finally skin starts peeling off. He steps out of the skin and is about to step into the healing pool only to look down and discover that he was still covered with hard rough scaly skin as before. Eustace tries a second and third time to remove the scaly skin. It is only when he, Eustace, allows Aslan to undress him that he finds the healing that he has been crying out for. To quote: "The very first tear He (Aslan/Jesus) made was so deep that I thought it had gone right into my heart. And when he began pulling the skin off, it hurt worse than anything I've ever felt. The only thing that made me able to bear it was just the pleasure of feeling the stuff peel off."[1]

That is how I envisioned my healing. God was peeling the layers of hurt, anger, bitterness, etc. off. I had tried my own methods of dealing with my heart, but my methods were not enough. It is only

1. Lewis, C. S. *The Voyage of the Dawn Treader*. Public Domain.

when we allow the Holy Spirit access (by taking down the defenses) to our heart that true healing can take place.

GETTING HONEST WITH YOURSELF

Are you willing to allow Aslan to undress you and heal you like my friend did who wrote this amazing letter to all of you many years ago? Are you willing to reconnect to your heart? Are you willing to feel your pain? Are you willing to peel back the scabs, the calluses, and let the dam collapse, releasing whatever is behind it? Are you willing to forgive yourself and others? As we describe defenses next, your decisions here will activate your free will and direct your heart in whatever direction you decide. Things will get messy! The well-defended heart looks proper, put together, confident, and well in control! The well-defended and dissociated heart feels that the world is predictable, and it operates as though it is on cruise control. Though others may have pointed out concerns about your relationships and the direction your life is taking, you may have fully convinced yourself that all is well. But chances are that is not completely true. You are missing out on the depths of God's love in your heart. Let things "get messy" and jump into "the healing pool!"

Are you willing to pull up the rug and see what may be behind that religious, controlled, and desensitized exterior that the world and even the church at times has produced? You will see that your heart is divided more than you think, and though with your mouth you confess that all is well and spiritually declare that Jesus is in control, you may see that there is a part of your will that has itself in full control, sitting in the driver's seat of your heart and keeping you comfortable while it actively works against God's full calling on your life! If you are willing to let the Holy Spirit "mess with your stuff" and stir the pot of your pain-filled heart, then count the cost before building the tower (Luke 14:28) and avoid the foolishness that this verse describes in those who begin but do not complete what they build.

I have often compared someone who starts the process of healing the emotional heart without walking out the whole process to a surgery patient who would want to get off the operating table without being closed up. It would be better not to start than to begin and stop before the procedure is complete. This surgery is much needed though!

Our hearts are to be as a house built on the rock, and we will need to retrieve them from the "sinking sands" our defense mechanisms have deceived us into using as our foundation (see Matthew 7). It is time to build our homes (symbolizing our hearts) on the rock of Jesus, having Him as our foundation and our protection.

Once our defense mechanisms are lowered, the healing of our emotional wounds can come pretty quickly. One of the tricks to getting started is in getting to know your heart enough to find that your problems are not what you think they are. Most of the time, what you think is the problem is really just the trigger. What you spend your time problem solving and worrying over are likely just places of historical pain that hurt just like a bruise on your body does when it is touched. The trigger is not the issue, but it sure can help you expose the issue that is causing the divided heart.

Chapter 4: God: Our Protector

I f we are going to talk about having an undivided heart, letting our carnal defense mechanisms go, and letting God be our true protector, we should explore for a moment what that means. What does it look like when we allow God to be our true protector? What is different about how we act when we are trusting Him as our protector? Many of us have been taught religiously that God is our protector, and on an intellectual level we believe that this is so. However, when it comes to the practicality of how often we use our defense mechanisms to protect us without consulting Him, it becomes clear that we really still rely on ourselves to be our protection. Many others, especially those who have endured strong emotional pain and trauma, have an extremely difficult time reconciling the idea that God is their protector with the pain of their experience. Talk to anyone like this, and this legitimate question is posed, "If God is my protector then where was He when _____ happened?"

Where was He when your trauma happened? Both the divided and undivided heart can talk about these questions. It is not blasphemy to let your heart ask the tough questions. In fact, it's quite healthy and biblical. Ask your potential Protector (God), "Where were You when _____ happened?" It is OK to do so. Job did! Scripture says regarding Job that he was without sin (Job 1:22). If you are secure enough in your friendships, you can ask them the tough questions in your heart, so why not in your relationship with God? In my counseling office, many people have had the courage to talk and pray about their tougher questions with God, and they often get direct revelation from Him that He was with them, even seeing pictures of where He was and what He was doing. He helps them make sense of it all, and He wants to do the same thing for you!

God is not intimidated by our questions, nor is He angry or punitive about them. He actually welcomes them. Instead of making a holy crusade out of getting people to give lip service to a God they don't know as their safe protector yet, it is best to help them walk through their questions and thoughts without being judgmental. When my clients say they are angry at God and ask why He did not stop their pain, I can answer sincerely, "I don't know, but we sure can ask Him." I love them no matter what their beliefs are, and I allow the Holy Spirit and their divided, angry, and hurt hearts to lead our discussions. When they do begin exploring, I celebrate their journey, no matter where it takes them. It's in the safety and freedom of being able to explore our spiritual beliefs that we can be honest about our confusion. It is in this safety where we can admit to ourselves that we have not felt protected by God at times.

I am not intimidated to let people have an Elijah moment such as we see in 1 Kings 18 where God gives the people a time to compare Him to their gods and Elijah confronts his countrymen. If you remember this passage, you will recall that Elijah set up one altar to Jehovah God and the prophets of Baal built one to their god. Elijah was completely confident, as I am, that when the people compared the two gods, they would say "the Lord is God." Elijah put his sacrifice on an altar to God while the other prophets put a sacrifice on their altar to Baal to test which god was real, which god was powerful, and which god would respond:

> *"You call on the name of your god, and I will call on the name of the Lord. The god who answers by fire—he is God"* (1 Kings 18:24).

> *"Then the fire of the Lord fell and consumed the burnt sacrifice, and the wood and the stones and the dust, and it licked up the water that was in the trench. Now*

God: Our Protector

when all the people saw it, they fell on their faces; and they said, 'The Lord, He is God! The Lord, He is God!'" (1 Kings 18:38-39 NKJV).

There was no comparison! The god Baal had no response, and the Lord not only answered with fire from heaven but burned up the entire altar, showing Himself plainly to be all powerful like none other! When we, with an open heart, give Him the chance to show Himself for who He really is, He will always show that there are none that compare to Him.

Our God is a strong God, a powerful God, a good protector, a faithful guide. He is a good Father, an over-protective Father, watching our every move and our every thought. He is *"closer than a brother"* (Proverbs 18:24 NKJV) and has only the best plans for us. One of my favorite Scriptures that shows the heart of our God as our protector is Psalm 91. This psalm is a daily comfort, a strong weapon to help us fight against fear; it's also a good foundation for building our faith in God who is our true and only Protector. Psalm 91 challenges us to give up being our own protector and allow the One who is truly able to do the job. Many have used this Scripture in times of physical and emotional trouble. Read Psalm 91, and pay attention to how reading this chapter affects your heart:

Psalm 91

"Whoever dwells in the shelter of the Most High will rest in the shadow of the Almighty. I will say of the Lord, 'He is my refuge and my fortress, my God, in whom I trust.'

Surely he will save you from the fowler's snare and from the deadly pestilence. He will cover you with his feathers, and under his wings you will find refuge; His faithfulness will be your shield and rampart.

You will not fear the terror of night, nor the arrow that flies by day, Nor the pestilence that stalks in the darkness, nor the plague that destroys at midday.

The Journey into the Divided Heart

A thousand may fall at your side, ten thousand at your right hand, but it will not come near you. You will only observe with your eyes and see the punishment of the wicked.

If you say, 'The Lord is my refuge,' and you make the Most High your dwelling, no harm will overtake you, no disaster will come near your tent. For he will command his angels concerning you to guard you in all your ways; they will lift you up in their hands, so that you will not strike your foot against a stone.

You will tread on the lion and the cobra; you will trample the great lion and the serpent. 'Because he loves me,' says the Lord, 'I will rescue him; I will protect him, for he acknowledges my name.'

He will call on me, and I will answer him; I will be with him in trouble, I will deliver him and honor him. With long life I will satisfy him and show him my salvation.'"

What a powerful text! I have been reassured by this passage many times when I have been in the middle of trials. It has been a great help to my clients too, as they deal with their many triggers and traumas that are at the root of their pain. Reading this psalm will not take away all our fears and emotional pain like some panacea. God's protection doesn't give us a perfect life. God still lets us feel pain, but just as a child learns life lessons and matures through decision-making by sometimes experiencing pain, so do we as adults. As it says in the passage, *"I (God) will be with him (you) in trouble."* The truth in this psalm brings a peace to my spirit that is much more powerful than any fears in my soul. There is such a place of rest *"in the shadow of the Most High."* If you have experienced it, you will never be the same. We do not need our own defenses when we say, *"He is my refuge and my fortress."* Turn back and read Psalm 91 again, but this time make it personal by changing the pronouns a bit. Doing this will help you feel God's presence, especially since He wrote it *directly to you.*

Isn't that psalm amazing? Many of you just felt the presence of God as your protector while reading that! When He is with you and you are able to let your heart sense Him as your protector, you will not need all of the defense mechanisms that we are about to study.

In order to experience God's safety and peace as your protector, you must learn to be mindful of what's happening inside of you when you are in His presence. While reading this psalm, some of you may have sensed some tension inside, even a sudden headache, tightness of jaw, muscle tension, and possibly stress, irritability, depression, or sadness. If you didn't read Psalms 91 with your name in it, please do so now. God's Word exposes what is already inside of you, just like turning on the light exposes what was in the dark.

When reading the psalm, some of you felt a real peace and rest. If you look at this peacefulness more closely, you find it is a contentment deeper than your words can express. It's like the old hymn that says, "It is well with my soul." Contentment in God's presence comes when we realize that He is with us, and when we read the *"living and active"* Word of God, we feel that He is close and realize we are safe and secure (Hebrews 4:12 NASB). When you feel His love wash over you, it becomes much easier to let Him be your everyday protector. For those of you who do not often feel God's presence like this, or who experienced nothing when reading Psalm 91, you may have some defense mechanisms that are blocking your heart from feeling His presence just like they block you from feeling close to people in your life. Maybe some of you felt anger—that is OK. Maybe some of you felt cynical and negative. The Word of God is powerful. You can look at where this anger and resistance is coming from and make further decisions from there. This is all part of the process of healing a divided heart.

Too often, we are reliant on our intellect, but true relationship is fostered only by a heart encounter with God. Maybe you have known *of* God but not had a real encounter *with* God, and this is why you're being your own protector. If so, you might want to ask God right now to reveal Himself to you, and see what happens. Maybe He will show you that He is a much better Protector of your heart than you ever could be. He can give you His peace that surpasses your understanding (Phil. 4:7) as well as your anxiety and your depression. Give it a try by asking

God silently right now, "Will You reveal Yourself to me as my Great Protector?" Write down what you see, feel, and hear:

_____

_____

_____

_____

Lots of people struggle with asking why God has not protected them. They fail to realize that there is another player in the picture of why we suffer so much on planet earth. If you believe that there is a God, then maybe you believe that there is also a devil that is also moving about the earth. There is an enemy that is really to blame for the evil that is happening all around. I'm not talking about the red guy with the pitch fork in the cartoons; I am talking about the being that the Word of God says comes as a wolf in sheep's clothing (Matthew 7:15) to *"steal, and to kill, and to destroy"* (John 10:10 NKJV). Maybe he has something to do with the evil in this world and the harm that has come to you in life. God is a good protector, but we have to discern when there is a wolf in our midst. We have to fight and protect against him with an undivided heart.

The interesting thing is that the Devil (if you believe he exists) gets off scot free as if he had no part in the horrible evil that people often blame God for. I understand it when people just don't believe in a spiritual realm at all. I understand when they believe that there is no heaven or hell, no God and no Devil. Maybe that is how they were taught or just where they landed in their beliefs, but isn't it interesting that those that believe the Bible is God's Word, which mentions the word *Devil* 57 times and *Satan* 49, often struggle to believe that the Devil really exists? The Barna poll on U.S. religious belief taken in 2001 showed this trend plainly when it said, "The notion that Satan, or the devil, is a real being who can influence people's lives is regarded as hogwash by most Americans. Only one-quarter (27 percent) strongly believes that Satan is real while a majority argues that he is merely a symbol of evil."[2] Mormons (59 percent) and Assembly of God believers (56 percent) are most likely to accept the reality of Satan's existence while Catholics, Lutherans, Episcopalians, and Methodists are the least likely (less than 22 percent of those polled).

Maybe you are part of the 73 percent of Christians who don't believe that there is a devil, if so, then this is an important question to answer for yourself, especially when considering whether or not God is a good Protector. God's protection is like any good security alarm in your house—it still has to be turned on through prayer, still has to be used properly through His Word, and you still have to be aware that you have an enemy, the Devil. We have to learn to use God's ways as our security system and learn how to call out to Him, just as we need to know how to call out to the police when the security alarm goes off. I encourage you to also look into the biblical truth that there is a devil and to learn how to use God's security system to fight against him because he is the ultimate cause of your trauma.

Learning how to walk in a relationship with God as our protector comes from relating to Him and building trust in Him. Noticing how you feel, as you did when reading Psalm 91, is an indicator of your trust level. There are many ways to build trust. How do we do this when counseling people? The Immanuel prayer model is one great ministry tool that helps people get started on this journey. It is taught by Dr. Karl Lehman. *Immanuel* means "God with us" and is a ministry tool that according to their website at immanuualapproach.com[3] says: *"Our ultimate goal with the Immanuel approach for life is getting to the place where we perceive the Lord's presence, and abide in an interactive connection with Jesus, as our usual, normal, baseline condition as we walk through life each day. In therapy/ministry sessions as well as in everyday life, the first, number one, highest priority item on the agenda is to be with God."*

2. Barna Research Group, Ltd. "Religious Beliefs Vary Widely By Denomination." Barna Research Online. June 25, 2001. Accessed December 01, 2016. http://www.barna.org.

3. Immanuel Approach. Accessed December 01, 2016. http://www.immanuelapproach.com/biblical-basis/.

The Journey into the Divided Heart

Oftentimes when our clients are open to this ministry, we direct them to just ask God to show them a time when God, Jesus, or the Holy Spirit was with them. As they meditate, they will often be reminded of a time when they felt really close to Him, they recall His goodness, and they are able to access the emotions of that moment. Perceiving the Lord's presence as your protector must go much deeper than an intellectual belief or set of thoughts, which is why this model is so important. You will appreciate Him so much, and should verbalize this to Him and to others as you have your own Immanuel moment! I encourage you to try an "Immanuel Moment" right now by praying, "Holy Spirit, will You show me a time when You were close to me and being my Protector?" Write down any memories or pictures you get below and give Him thanks.

_____

_____

_____

_____

I encourage you to also meditate on the following Scriptures as you embark on the process of healing your divided heart. They will be a great encouragement as you consider making God your true and only protector:

"Turn your ear to me, come quickly to my rescue; be my *rock of refuge, a strong fortress to save me"* (Psalms 31:2).

"Bow down Your ear to me, deliver me speedily; be my rock of refuge, a fortress of defense to save me" (Psalms 31:2 NKJV).

"You have been a refuge for the poor, a refuge for the needy in his distress, a shelter from the storm and a shade from the heat. For the breath of the ruthless is like a storm driving against a wall" (Isaiah 25:4).

God: Our Protector

"The Lord of hosts is with us; the God of Jacob is our refuge" (Psalms 46:11 NKJV).

"He alone is my rock and my salvation; he is my fortress, I will never be shaken" (Psalms 62:2).

"He alone is my protector and deliverer. He is my refuge; I will not be upended" (Psalms 62:2 NET).

"O God, my God, to thee do I watch at break of day. For thee my soul hath thirsted; for thee my flesh, O how many ways!" (Psalms 62:2 Douay-Rheims).

"He will not allow your foot to be moved; He who keeps you will not slumber" (Psalms 121:3 NKJV).

"Be my strong refuge, to which I may resort continually; You have given the commandment to save me, for You are my rock and my fortress" (Psalms 71:3 NKJV).

"Behold, He who keeps Israel shall neither slumber nor sleep" (Psalms 121:4 NKJV).

"The Lord of hosts is with us; the God of Jacob is our refuge" (Psalms 46:7 NKJV).

"O Israel, trust in the Lord; He is their help and their shield. O house of Aaron, trust in the Lord; He is their help and their shield. You who fear the Lord, trust in the Lord; He is their help and their shield" (Psalms 115:9-11 NKJV).

"For you were like sheep going astray, but have now returned to the Shepherd and Overseer of your souls" (1 Peter 2:25 NKJV).

The Journey into the Divided Heart

DEFENDING OUR HEARTS AGAINST GOD

Why would we defend our hearts against a loving God who is on our side? We don't mean to do it, but we do nevertheless. One of the saddest states I have found in believers is being stuck in defense mechanisms when they are unaware that these defenses are even operating. These good-hearted believers often feel attacked when others bump into their walls or when someone points out that they have these defenses. They just feel further attacked when they cannot see (and possibly do not want to see) the "walls" that they have erected around themselves. At this point they will activate their defenses, even unconsciously, and further distance themselves from anyone who would confront them or try to help them. They will feel attacked if confronted—even in love—and will resist the voice of Holy Spirit who is active in convicting us when we are acting and thinking outside of the will of God. The Lord is not trying to punish them at all. He wants to protect and lead us toward His blessings! Unfortunately when a person has these defense mechanisms operating in their hearts, God's voice of conviction is too often actively guarded against. The believer feels as though they are being attacked, when actually he or she is really being loved. As the Word of God says, *"For the Lord disciplines those he loves, and he punishes each one he accepts as his child"* (Hebrews 12:6 NLT). When these convictions are shut down and guarded against, we have a baby Christian who will not allow himself to be disciplined and taught to grow up into maturity of character in the faith.

At the risk of theologically triggering your defenses against me and the rest of the content of this book, I will say to you today that our God is a very personable God who speaks to His people regularly through all kinds of media, not just through the Bible. He literally speaks to us all day long. Our God is a very intimate God, who seeks to lead us into all truth (John 16:13). He truly is a shepherd to us, His sheep, and desires to lead us beside still waters and comfort our souls (Psalms 23:2). This type of relational, conversational, and deeply personal lifestyle with God is a rarity in much of the Christian church today. Many are living in times such as those of Samuel where it was said:

God: Our Protector

"Meanwhile, the boy Samuel served the Lord by assisting Eli. Now in those days messages from the Lord were very rare, and visions were quite uncommon"
(1 Samuel 3:1 NLT).

If you read this passage in context of the season that Samuel was living in, you will realize that this lack of visions and communication from God was directly related to the rebellion and lack of conviction of God's leaders who were not vigilant to keep sin from entering the temple. It wasn't only the prostitution that was happening inside the temple walls itself that was being addressed by God either. The focus of God's wrath was directed toward their passivity (a common defense mechanism used at God's expense much more than most of us are aware of). Eli, who was the priest of that day, was passively watching sin take place without taking action against his sons who were defiling the house of the Lord. It's likely that Eli was passive because he was avoiding conflict in his family. We believers are now the house of the Lord, and our passivity has the potential to hinder our ability to hear from God personally. Passivity is a powerful defense that will divide our hearts quickly!

God is ready to speak to His people today. A very important part of the believer's salvation is that they be able to have a direct relationship and ongoing conversation with God, not only on a daily basis but on an hour-by-hour basis. We need to hear direction from God throughout the day. This does not have to be spooky or super-spiritual either. It can, but does not have to, come in a vision like Daniel's (Daniel 2:19), or in a thundering voice from an angel. Our communication happens with God in our spirits, because He is a Spirit! Our direction from God comes to us most often as a *"still small voice"* (1 Kings 19:12) heard in our hearts at about the same volume as our own thoughts. But if our spirit is broken, then what? If our heart is split, how will we hear well? If our spirit is divided from itself, how can we function properly in our relationship with God? If our spirit (our heart) is walled off from God and others because of its defense mechanisms, then we are often unable to connect to the voice of our Lord. Just as a radio will not be able to pick up a frequency if it is disconnected from its antenna, so our hearts are the receivers of all that God is speaking to us moment by moment.

DISCERNMENT: LETTING GOD'S VOICE PROTECT US

Discernment should be an every-day, every-minute part of the believer's life. It happens on a heart and relational level with God. *Discernment* means to step back and separate, meaning to be able to recognize God's voice speaking to you in your heart and separate from the defense mechanisms, the thoughts, and the emotions of the soul. This process looks like this:

> *"For the word of God is living and powerful, and sharper than any two-edged sword, piercing even to the division of soul [our mind, will, and emotions] and spirit...and is a discerner of the thoughts and intents of the heart"* (Hebrews 4:12 NKJV).

Just as Jesus did "nothing" without knowing the Father's will (John 5:19), so can I do nothing without Him. I can discern in my spirit what I am to do. I can know when to share openly with others and when it is not safe. I can know God's will for my schedule, and for large and small decisions that lead me through life, down the narrow path the Bible talks about (Matthew 7:14). Do not let your mind and the defense mechanisms within you oversimplify, minimize, and numb you to this truth. Most of us have a very long way to go before we can truly say that we discern each decision that we make during our day. If God is to be our protector though, we need to be operating in this close communication with Him on a daily basis. Taking an inventory of all your defenses is a great step in weeding out the hindrances that inhibit your communication with others, with knowing yourself, and with hearing from your Father God. Let's get started!

Chapter 5: Defense Mechanisms: the Carnal Mind's Attempts to Control Pain

F or some of you, the very mention of defense mechanisms brings a bad taste to your mouth because it has a psychological connotation. Some might accuse me of speaking "psycho-babble" at the very mention of it. In many instances, I would agree, but I have learned that there is a need to minister and teach regarding both the spiritual and natural realms. Using the names of defense mechanisms that psychology has labeled is a huge help in understanding our own hearts.

The labeling and defining of defense mechanisms dates back to Freudian psychoanalysis in the 1936 writing by Anna Freud titled *The Ego and the Mechanisms of Defense.* We have been using this term and studying these psychological tendencies ever since. Many Christians throw out the baby with the bathwater and don't want to talk or read about such secular things as defense mechanisms or look at any emotional interventions that are not found directly in the Bible. This is why, for some, the very idea of Christian counseling is controversial. Some suggest that God is the only way to address your negative emotions, and that all we need to do is pray more and read our Bibles more when we feel anxious and depressed. While this is certainly helpful, we often throw out helpful understandings and writings because they came from men like Freud, whom many in the Christian church consider to be humanistic and even an occultist. All wisdom is given by God though, and is useful in context of the Scriptures for the common good of man.

> *"For the Lord gives wisdom, from his mouth come knowledge and understanding"* (Proverbs 2:6 NKJV).

As we launch into this important understanding of our tendencies to insulate ourselves from emotional pain and the different defenses we use to do that, please realize that just as secular scholars have mapped out various accurate scientific and medical theories and laws that explain God's physical creation, secular scholars have also learned a great deal about our defense mechanisms and the human heart. Their work has aided us greatly in explaining how the natural and carnal sides of our being act when protecting themselves emotionally.

Psychology has not only benefited us by mapping out these defenses, but it has helped in giving us definitions of disorders and diagnoses that we can use to find interventions and common and predictable progressions that fit with each category. Counseling, both Christian and secular, benefits greatly from being able to gather information about mental health symptoms and use them to diagnose mental health issues. A correct diagnosis leads to a correct intervention. Some Christians have difficulty with this concept of using psychology in the process of leading someone to peace and a sound mind, and some feel personally labelled when words are given to their defenses or their symptoms. Just remember that *you are not your diagnosis.* You are not your defense mechanisms. They are something you deal with; they are not your identity. As I tell my kids who have an attention deficit disorder (ADD) diagnosis: It does not change who a person is if they are found to be near-sighted and need glasses, and so it is with ADD or any other diagnosis that the person has been given. They are still the person God created them to be. Their eyes just work in such a way that they can benefit from glasses, which are prescribed after diagnosing the problem.

Though psychology does have many approaches to treat the symptoms it categorizes, I believe that it is in the act of a loving God and in His power that there is true alleviation from these symptoms. We know this from the Scripture that states, *"Every good and every perfect gift is from above"* (James 1:17). Where psychology and the medical field are able to help us label, cope with, and find recovery for our mental health symptoms, only God is able to mend and heal completely by His power!

Defense mechanisms are our means of running from pain. Some defenses are hardwired into us; some are learned by observation; and others are directly taught to us by our teachers, parents, friends, and even pastors. If you are reading this book and have no knowledge of the emotional pain that you have suffered and still carry, then chances are you have multiple defense mechanisms operating inside you right now. Our tendency to run from emotional pain is almost as automatic as sneezing when we have a tickle, and until they are tracked our defense mechanisms will subconsciously operate on a heart level, leading us toward the destruction of our relationships and, when left unchecked, the stifling of our spiritual growth.

DEFENSE MECHANISMS: YOUR OWN PERSONAL BODYGUARDS

Picture with me, if you will, the analogy that having defense mechanisms is like having a bodyguard who stands watch around your heart day and night. This bodyguard does not say a whole lot, but he knows that his job is to protect, and protect he does! As you live and interact with the world around you, your bodyguard is there, keeping watch and prepared to use whatever measures at his disposal to help maintain your sense of security, safety, and peace. He has strategies to steer you away from potentially harmful situations that could lead to rejection, fear, or grief. The bodyguard has, as most do, a type of sixth sense that keeps him tuned in, like radar, to anyone or anything that may cause turmoil. Being good at his job, he is constantly taking in information and storing and analyzing what potential harm may be present, alerting you immediately when risk factors of emotional pain are high. However, just because we feel safe does not mean that we are.

The Journey into the Divided Heart

Sometimes we need to fire our bodyguards when they begin to insulate us from our environment in ways that keep us from living life as we ought.

A defense mechanism is like a well-fortified castle. This castle has thick walls and is armed to protect against any and all invaders who may come against you. The castle has a moat around it, and after entering the castle you (like most of us) close the drawbridge to any who represent any potential emotional harm. The bridge does not only separate you from those who may really hurt you, but also from all those who even look, act, or believe differently than you. I would say most of us may even have some pretty vicious-looking alligators that swim the waters around the castle where our hearts dwell, and they are ready to eat anyone alive who would potentially come against us! The problem is that when you are inside this protective stronghold, you may feel safe, but you are also unable to interact openly with anyone or anything that is outside of the castle walls. You are not only protected from harm, but you are protected from good too—like people, relationships, and any form of support. You feel safer with these walls up emotionally, but at some point you realize that they are actually making you live life completely alone. You are cut off from the highway that God uses to deliver provision and blessings into your life—which is your own heart. Is your castle a safe haven, or is it a prison? Is it bringing you all that you wanted in life, or is it prohibiting you from receiving what your heart wants and needs to be truly alive? These castle walls are breeding grounds for isolationism, prejudice, self-righteousness, and even hatred and delusional thinking about others. Hiding out in your castle can draw you back into the Dark Ages!

CHECKING YOUR BODYGUARDS AND EXPLORING YOUR CASTLE

The hardest part about sharing these examples is that many of your defense mechanisms were just activated! When I talk about emotional pain, your mind tells you that I am talking to that group of people who were sexually abused, tortured, physically beaten, or neglected. Through the process of minimizing, your mind is taking my words and keeping

58

you from applying them to yourself, even as you read! Your mind is insulating you from recognizing and identifying your own emotional pain in all of its forms and telling you, "This doesn't really apply to me," or "I don't really have that much pain." It uses denial to say, "I am OK," and projection to say, "This book would be great for my coworker who's gone through lots of trauma." Some of you may feel angry. You may suspect that I am trying to take you back to memories that may not be there or past hurts that you have already worked through. Your intellect will tell you, "I can't do anything about my past anyway," and your religiosity may even give you a Scripture to tell you to not ever think about the past or the hurts you have suffered.

So please, as you take the following inventory, beware of any hindrance or blockade to taking a true and honest look at the ways you guard your heart. Remember that knowing is half the battle, and gaining insight into how each of these defenses works within you will free you to make informed choices with an undivided heart.

> *I will give them an undivided heart and put a new spirit in them; I will remove from them their heart of stone and give them a heart of flesh* (Ezekiel 11:19).

TAKING INVENTORY

In the following chapters we will be taking a look at some of the main defense mechanisms. Become acquainted with them and watch and see how they operate in your heart. As you read, take an inventory of what you have been using to shield yourself from potential pain, rejection, hurt, and feelings of being out of control. The following is by no means a comprehensive list of all defense mechanisms, but rather those that God has highlighted for me to share with you. As you read, ask God to make these methods of self-protection clear to you and ask for His help in seeing how they operate in your heart. Some of these defenses are very active and some operate quietly and incognito but we all have them and use them every day—to our help and to our harm. Let's pray:

The Journey into the Divided Heart

*Father God, we thank You for the truth You have already brought to us as we read; our heart's desire and the decision of our free will is to ask You in humility to bring light to, and exposure to, all defenses inside of us that are hindering us from Your perfect will for our lives. We confess and admit that our defenses even right now are likely postured to divert us from Your revelation, so right now we declare Your sovereignty and the power of Your Holy Spirit to lead us into all truth and the personal application of this truth to our daily life. Open our eyes and our ears to see and hear all that You have for us without hindrance right now in Jesus' name, and give us the grace and courage to walk through our pain **with** You that it may be exposed underneath. Amen!*

Chapter 6: Anger

Anger is felt as an emotion, but it always comes second. Anger is a response to your pain. It surfaces through feelings of hurt, rejection, insecurity, and fear. The trick is to recognize anger as a defense and to get some revelation about what it is that triggered you into using this defense. Anger manifests in many different ways, and if you want to learn how to expose your heart further to let God's healing touch come in, you will need to get acquainted with how anger manifests itself in you.

Anger comes in many shapes and sizes—but we need to recognize that it is a defense used to protect ourselves from being vulnerable. Maybe you are the type who expresses anger aggressively by yelling, screaming, name calling, swearing, stomping, or throwing things. Maybe you even get violent and use physical force when you are angry. If you do, then you have a very strong defense mechanism that needs some serious attention. However, you are no more outside of the will of God than if you are the type of person who has anger they internalize and hide. The fact that it remains quiet does not diminish its power.

The Bible says, "Be angry and do not sin" (Ephesians 4:26 NKJV). I am a stuffer myself, but I am here to tell you that the "in-ee" people versus the "out-ee" people are both capable of hurting others equally when they manifest their anger toward others. Those that internalize their anger tend to isolate and punish others by giving them the silent treatment or by just becoming distanced and cold. These "internalizers" tend to keep a chip on their shoulder longer and keep a record of wrongs that they will hold like weapons to use against the others in their lives for years to come. Looks that could kill are common, and passive-aggressive behaviors that use avoidance and snubbing to get back at someone are no less filled with hate than slapping someone across the face.

We need to avoid minimizing our anger, referring to it as "just being a little upset," that is still anger. Call an ace an ace! We can classify ourselves as being "just a little miffed," "frustrated," or "ticked off," but these are all just watered down ways to say, "I am angry." Let's bring our anger into the light and call it what it is! Even if we do not act it out in violence or rage, anger is a feeling that has lots of actions that go with it. Some of these actions are aggressive, while others are passive.

I use the word *trigger* a lot when talking about anger because I am implying that whatever it is that set you off is not the main source of your emotions. Just like a trigger on a gun sets off an explosion that sends the bullet flying, certain circumstances in our lives set off explosions, and emotions can go flying and stirring within us. We should not be afraid of our angry feelings, but we should recognize that this anger, internalized or externalized, is a very active defense that can hurt people and divide our hearts just as much as a bullet can. The question isn't are you bad for being so angry, but what is happening underneath the anger? What pain are you going through that is leading to such a need to cover and protect?

If your anger is toward a person, try to grasp the truth that a person cannot "make" you feel anger or any other feeling for that matter. He or she can "trigger" or "touch a sore spot" in you that exposes feelings that are already there, but our anger is a choice that no one can force us into. Think of your past hurts and stored-up emotions as being kind of like a bruise on your heart. When you touch a bruise, it hurts. In fact, it can be very painful, but it is not the touch in itself that is the cause of the pain. That touch is triggering pain that came in through some previous trauma and has not healed yet. Think of the last time you stubbed your little toe in the middle of the night getting up to get a drink in the dark. Ouch! You went to bed and forgot about it—that is, until the moment you tried to put your socks and shoes on. That little part of your body, now black and blue, can bring you to your knees. No matter how careful you are with that bruised area, you are still going to feel lots of pain from the inflamed nerves and tissues that have not healed yet. It is not the sock or the shoe causing the pain. The sock is simply a trigger coming into contact with the unhealed pain that came from the prior trauma. It is the same with our hearts!

Anger can be an automatic reflex because, as you will learn in the intervention section, there is a whole part of your brain designated to instantly choose between "fight or flight" when there is perceived danger. Anger is most often a manifestation of the "fight" side of this reaction. Anger management programs and group therapies have been around for many decades, but some focus too much on angry behaviors and modifying behaviors to ensure that we act appropriately when angry. As with many other therapies, these short-term, bandage approaches to addressing internal heart issues leave a person shortchanged of the long-term help and healing that they want and deserve. We can normalize anger first by teaching people that anyone who is hit on the thumb with a hammer is likely to angrily shout out a curse word or two (yes, even you highly refined Christian people). The anger coming from the fight or flight side of your brain is really just showing us that you are in pain or that you feel you are in danger. It is the pain beneath the behaviors and symptoms that is the real problem, but it can be more work, feel more intense, and be much more difficult to deal with the roots of your anger. So, many people avoid the true roots and origins and focus only on modifying their behavior.

Ask yourself: Am I really mad at my boss, my spouse, my parents, my pastor, or is this a reflex in me that is indicating that there is a trigger point underneath it all because my heart is in pain? Look at the rejection, abandonment, grief, loss, and fear that you feel with these trigger point relationships in your life, and you will be able to get to the bottom of where you really need to heal. Angry behaviors are often just a distraction, a diversion away from where the real conversation needs to go. Some of the couples in my office love to fight. They think yelling is their primary love language. It is where they feel most comfortable with themselves. It is a communication comfort zone. By yelling and belittling each other, they can hide their divided hearts from vulnerability. Bantering and debating diverts them from the things they really need and want to talk about.

Parents often bite on the bait of the angry behaviors in their kids. They are just a diversion, and it is not helpful to address only these behaviors. Unfortunately, many adults don't know an alternative way to address these angry emotions. They end up fighting their child's anger with their own anger. We fight fire with fire! "Don't raise your voice at me, young man," we scream, leaving our kids without a model of how to truly handle their own anger. Neither do they recognize it as a defense mechanism in them. We get so busy addressing the angry behaviors in our kids that we miss the pain that is happening internally, which when addressed is our only true means of alleviating the negative patterns they are stuck in. Maybe your angry kid is really a scared kid. Maybe your angry kid is actually an insecure kid and feeling like they don't fit in or don't measure up with their peers. Maybe they are going through some sort of trauma and you don't even know about it. Maybe the kid inside of you is just like that too, and you need to look at where you are scared, feel like you don't measure up, or don't fit in.

Anger is one of the primary defense mechanisms that our hearts use to protect ourselves, and it manifests in many different ways. Sometimes anger is the result of lacking a legitimate need that God did put there in your heart, but the way that your anger is going about trying to get that need met is counterproductive. Maybe you need a listening ear, but you don't know how to express your needs in a way that will get them met. Learn how to say, "I am really upset right now and could really use some time to vent to you, dear." Or even better: "I am really hurt right now and could really use a hug please." Expressing your true needs is a big part of anger management. Once you find out what these needs truly are and where they are coming from inside of you, you are that much closer to having those needs met.

There is also an anger that is called righteous anger, which is always accompanied by love, peace, and joy. This righteous anger does not arise out of a self-protective and reactive stance. Sometimes the anger you feel is the same anger that God is feeling at some sin that is happening to you or around you. God hates sin, and yet He still loves the sinner—even you and me! Your job is not to eradicate all the injustice in this world though. Your first job is to get to know how your anger manifests, what your trigger points are, and what needs you have that are not being met. Often you will find bruises behind your anger that are still unhealed from the past. Your anger is the red flag telling you that the time is now to heal these bruises up! If anger is at all dividing your heart, it is time to be more mindful of it. Answering the following questions may help.

1. How does your anger usually manifest? Are you more of an in-ee or an out-ee angry person?

_____

_____

_____

_____

2. What are your main trigger points for anger, and what do these tell you about the origin of your pain? (For instance, "when people touch me"—maybe you were touched in a wrong manner in the past?)

_____

_____

_____

_____

3. What emotional "bruises" do you have that have left you sensitive and have resulted in you using anger to hide?

_____

_____

_____

_____

4. Are you willing to acknowledge that it is your decision to be angry every time this feeling surfaces?

_____

_____

_____

_____

Chapter 7: Avoidance

Most defense mechanisms have an element of avoidance in them. There is an element of biological programming inside of us that leads us to this particular defense. Avoidance is often the flight side of that "fight or flight response" that we were talking about earlier. The flight response to fear and threat has been well documented in psychology and is programmed into our autonomic nervous system. When triggered with any level of fear, our brain heightens and gives off an automatic release of adrenaline to the body, increasing our heart rate, constricting our blood vessels, and heightening our senses, so that we are physically prepared to fight any threat or run like the wind to get away from it. All that is required to activate this avoidance "flight response" is the perception that harm is near, and we find hundreds of ways to avoid anything that resembles the appearance of what has hurt us in the past. Our flight program is not just activated against perceived physical harm, but emotional and relational harm as well.

Avoidance of any situation is related to fear, and when this element of our autonomic nervous system is activated, we tend to operate in a hyperactive reactive state that only magnifies the perceived fears that triggered the cycle inside of us. Fear, even small and undetected, can trigger this flight program, which automatically tells us how to stay clear of even the smallest discomfort by avoidance. It will provide a solution to just about any challenge through running away! The problem with this is that when we use avoidance we are also missing out on getting help from others. We need help getting back to what they call homeostasis—the state of being physically and emotionally calm and feeling safe.

Anything that you go out of your way to not experience is an avoidance reaction to fear. Your way of defending against that fear is avoidance, and this needs to be addressed and healed. You can do all things through Christ who gives you strength (Philippians 4:13), and you can do it all with love, joy, peace, and all the fruit of the spirit of God (Galatians 5:22-23). Many people think that they don't have fears and anxiety "like those other people" in the world, but the reason they don't experience fear and anxiety is because they avoid everything that would challenge them. There are fears that are healthy and hardwired in us to avoid particular situations for the sake of survival, but common areas of avoidance like public speaking, confronting others, taking risks in relationships, leading others confidently, problem solving stressful situations, and being emotionally vulnerable with others you feel have hurt you are very necessary to a healthy and happy life. Whatever it is you are doing, if avoidance is the motive then it needs to stop! Avoidance is not coming from the true you or from God's heart. Instead, it may be an unchecked defense mechanism that is leading you astray and stealing God's blessing from your life. In your avoidance, you may be missing out on revelations of who God really created you to be, and Romans 8:37 says you are "*more than a conqueror!*"

There are many examples in Scripture of people who used avoidance. Jonah ran away and avoided Nineveh and God's will (Jonah 1-5); Moses wanted to avoid Pharaoh because of his insecurity about his ability to speak (Exodus 4:14). Eli avoided confronting his sons who were priests and was disciplined by God (1 Samuel 2-4), and Peter avoided potential harm by denying Jesus three times (John 18:15). There are many more. Here are some examples from my life, and I encourage you to think of times and places in your life when you have avoided something or someone. This defense mechanism is one of the most common to all of us. I was the kid in class, all through elementary school, who when asked to give a book report or speech was terrified. I used avoidance by slumping in my chair as the teacher took volunteers. Being the last to go forward put even more pressure on me as I compared myself to all the others. (Why didn't all of us learn to volunteer first when we were anxious to get it over with?) I was also shy when wanting to play with others on the playground, and later in life would shy away from asking out whatever girl I thought was cute. When I look back, I can now see that avoidance stole experiences from me, but that was all I knew.

Of course this fear continued past high school and through college, right up to the time I became a professional in the field of social work. Public speaking opportunities often presented themselves, but with avoidance wholly ingrained in my thought process and behaviors, the automatic answer to such requests was always: "No, not me" and "I am more of the behind-the-scenes kind of a guy." The scariest thing about this defense and others is that I had defined myself by this set of behaviors and self-protective measures, and the more I described myself as a shy, introverted, behind-the-scenes kind of a guy, the more I actually believed it! I thought this was my personality, the way God made me. Others began to define me this way too, not out of ill will toward me but out of what they saw on the surface versus my real identity. My character, my personality, my entire picture of who I was, was revolving around this avoidance mechanism, which was not allowing me to see all that I truly was in Christ.

I was finally able to hear "the rest of the story" when I learned to truly hear the voice of my Creator who confronted my thinking in love. After I had turned down a speaking engagement, I remember clearly hearing God say to me, "Steve, you think you are shy and introverted, but you are not." I did what many of you do also. I proceeded to tell God why He was wrong in order to help Him see what he was missing. (Sorry, God!) I reported confidently to God that I never really liked talking to groups of people, that I was uncomfortable speaking in crowds, and that I loved to serve where I didn't need to be noticed. I even tried to help God see that my family and many of my friends were the same way. I proceeded to tell Him that much of this "shyness" was likely just how He made me. I'm sure He had a good laugh at all of this, and I can now too.

The Journey into the Divided Heart

You can see where this is going, can't you? How wrong I was! It took God only a few sentences to point out that I was not shy but that I just avoided potential discomfort because I was afraid. God blew a hole in my lifelong theory about who I was and said, "Son, you are not shy or introverted; you just have a spirit of fear (2 Timothy 1:7) that manifests in avoidance of anything frightening; and you have defined your personality around this spiritual stronghold." Wow! That was a hard one to take, and it has been even harder to walk out. I am still learning to walk that out in many ways, but I can tell you that today there is not much that brings me more joy than bringing a message to a body of believers, leading worship, meeting new people, and being on the front lines of what God is doing. How exhilarating all these things are to me now that my divided heart is healing! They almost got stolen from me through my belief in a lie about myself that centered on a single defense mechanism called avoidance.

Avoidance is a powerful defense mechanism that is often very subtle as well as generational. Avoidance is often normalized and can even become a part of the way you define your personality, as it did in my case. It can be validated as a normal response to feeling anxious and afraid, but it needs to be confronted for what it is. It is a defense mechanism of "flight" used to insulate us from pain and deny all that God made us to be. Taking risks is necessary, and as Joyce Meyers says, "Do it afraid!" Doing what you would normally avoid is important to overcoming your root fears beneath so you can have the freedom you deserve! Journaling time!

1. What type of situations do you tend to avoid?

_____

_____

_____

_____

70

Avoidance

2. What are you afraid of that may lead you to the "flight response"?

_____

_____

_____

_____

3. How might your life change if you gave up avoidance in these areas?

_____

_____

_____

_____

4. How do you think your definition of yourself might change if you stopped avoiding these areas of your life?

_____

_____

_____

_____

5. In what areas of avoidance are you willing to start "doing it afraid"?

_____

_____

_____

_____

ADDICTION IS A SOLUTION TO A PAIN
OR PROBLEM.

ADDICTION looks FOR THE IMMEDIATE
RESULT, OR ESCAPE

PORN + SEX ADDICTION SHAME BASED

JOURNAL WENT TEMPTED, EXAMINE
WHAT THE HEART WILL TELL YOU

Chapter 8: Addictions

Addictions are not often listed in psychology textbooks as a defense mechanism, but addictions can definitely be a form of them. Like any other defense mechanisms, we can look at the motive for any action or thought pattern and see that the purpose for using alcohol, drugs, and any other addiction can be to escape emotional pain. There is definitely a physical component to the addiction cycle that brings with it additional complications, but let's look at what we are really desiring when we open that refrigerator over and over, when we are drawn to pornography on the Internet, and, no less damaging, when we overwork ourselves compulsively (being a workaholic). These addictions provide a "solution" or a perceived way out of negative emotions.

Think about it. When pot smokers smoke a joint, they are going to induce a calming and numbing of their emotions, relieving anxiety, worry, and fear. When drinkers begin to feel that buzz from drinking a few beers, there is a lowering of inhibitions, allowing them to briefly feel free to express their emotions and to act in a way that makes them feel like their true selves. The pornography addict usually gets a sense of brief euphoria, or a rush, that quickly yields to shame and the need for greater levels of perversity to satisfy itself. Though the consequences of most addictions are costly, there's always a payoff to an addiction that makes it feel worth it at the time, no matter how destructive that substance or activity may be to you and your family. In my office I have people picture a set of old-fashioned scales, and as much as the consequences weigh on one side of the scales, the decision to use that addiction shows us that the addicted person sees the benefits to their behavior as even greater, or weighing more, in that moment than anything else. An addiction can bring a sort of delusion and skews our thinking drastically. The addict needs to see the payoffs of their different addiction to see what their heart is really in need of. The benefits that you think you are gaining from the addictions in your life are what makes it worth risking paying the high price that your addiction brings with it.

When considering the legal ramifications, for example, of drinking, what could the payoff be? You could go to jail for drunk driving, lose your job, get separated or divorced from your spouse, feel lots of guilt and shame, have financial hardship, and also feel you have to hide all the time. What could the payoffs be of using heroin or crack cocaine, which are definitely life threatening and risky to one's job, relationships, and finances? You can become physically addicted and dependent on many substances, but there are emotional draws to the addiction also. The payoff (at least in part) that makes all these risks worthwhile to you is that the addiction is giving you a way to stop feeling your negative feelings. It is a defense, a wall around your heart, a solution (though a poor one) that acts as if it's giving you relief from negative emotions.

Psychology calls this concept self-medicating. As you take in a substance or any other form of addiction, just as you would take a painkiller to ease the pain from a headache, there is an easing of your emotional pain. The problem is that these addictions always bring on more of a headache and mask the true emotions that are behind the headaches all the more. A painkiller could mask the headache pain from a brain tumor for all we know, so we need to feel the pain to assess it. Addictions are the way humans attempt to "feel better" and mostly cover the symptoms rather than exposing the root of what is happening internally.

Apart from the typical addictions to substances that we think of, there are additional categories of addictions that are just as powerful and dangerous. Consider codependency. Simply defined, codependency is an addiction to people. The codependent person needs to be needed and wants to be wanted on a compulsive level that often leads them

74

to enable or make it easy for others to continue with their addictions. These "enablers" help others continue in their negative behaviors inadvertently because they have to keep these other persons whom they *need* around them to make them feel good. The perfectionist and the overachiever both are addicted to always doing more, striving, and working compulsively, but usually they are afraid to either fail or be judged as having failed by themselves or others. Talk about causing anxiety and eventual hopelessness! Sexual addictions are hugely pervasive, as are approval addictions (needing to be liked by everyone), and addictions to dieting, working out, and other activities that seem healthy but are harmful when done in excess.

As you read about addictions, please be aware that defenses such as denial, rationalization, and minimizing go hand in hand with them. The key to defenses is that they are working unconsciously (most of the time) to keep you from feeling. This means that even doing an inventory of your addictions will bring up defenses that protect you from feeling guilty, bad, convicted, or shamed by your own thoughts. When we begin to inventory our defenses and allow God to shine His light on these different coping mechanisms and walls in our hearts, this can itself often triggers those defenses further, intensifying the need to hide. They then, in effect, shield us from any insights that may lead us into the loving conviction we need.

Here are a few more subtle yet still very destructive addictions that you may not notice:

- Workaholism: The addiction of working compulsively and excessively. From a family's perspective, this is very damaging because it rejects and abandons them. The family suffers the loss of time and attention from the breadwinner of the family who is away more than God would want them to be.

- Entertainment Addiction. In the church, we often discuss the sin of pornography, but what about the romance novels, the TV shows, the movies, and every other form of entertainment that we rely on to help us retreat to a fantasy life so we can get our minds off the realities that push and pressure us internally. "It's just entertainment!" many would say, but can entertainment become an addiction? Certainly! We have to assess the role these habits play in our lives emotionally, including when we use them and why we use them to discern if they are addictions or not.

- Materialism: The addiction to material objects and possessions in place of what is truly valuable. What about shopping and having to have the most up-to-date device or fashion that comes out on the market? Aren't these behaviors evidence of addictions? Yes, they are! When we do something to build a sense of self-worth and identity or to forget about the stress in our lives, or when we look at anything as the very source of our happiness, then this coping skill will lead to destruction, and yes, it is an addiction.

The emotional pain that addictions hide is often buried and repressed. We may be totally and completely unaware of what is hidden inside. The book of Proverbs says that "*the purposes of a man's heart are deep waters*" (Proverbs 20:5); this means that understanding our own motives and emotions is like trying to see a penny in the deep end of a swimming pool. We might see a very small shadow, but mostly it is hidden from our sight. A sure way to expose what may be "in the deep end" of your heart is to stop whatever you think may be an addiction in your life. Consider stopping whatever activity may be acting as a defense mechanism in your life for three full weeks and you will learn a lot about the role that addiction is playing and the emotions that it is covering. As you "avoid your avoidance" for this time, do some journaling and track what you feel right before the urge that you have to act out your addiction. These feelings will point to the root problems you have been trying to avoid.

Addictions can be very subtle. I had a client named Jane. She was always busy. In fact, Jane was never not busy. She could find something to do when there was nothing to do. She got a lot of work done, helped out her friends and neighbors more than most, and seemed on top of everything in her life. The problem was that Jane was experiencing anxiety and panic attacks. I sensed that her addiction to busyness was the cap on the bottle of her heart. Under that cap, a great deal of hidden pressure was trying to burst forth! I challenged her to go home, turn off the phone and the TV, and get rid of all distractions. That was her assignment for counseling. After avoiding this particular homework assignment for three months, Jane was able to sit and be still for five to ten minutes.

A remarkable and yet painful thing happened to Jane in that ten minutes. While sitting and being still in her apartment one day, Jane had some memories surface in her heart; they were pretty tough for her to bear. Jane's heart was exposed and the root of the pain and the origin of her deepest hurt was uncovered. Jane told me of a time in her childhood when she had plans to spend time with a young friend. Jane had to cancel her plans with her, and later learned that her friend had tragically died in a fire with the rest of her family at the house where she was supposed to go and play that same day. Jane finally let her heart remember and feel that day so far in the past. What a horrific set of emotions she faced! She was very brave. As she shared this with me, we found a vicious thought that had been plaguing her unbeknownst to her ever since that time. In asking her to describe the thinking behind the pain and grief she had suffered through for over thirty years, she said, "I should have been there, Steve; I could have saved my friend! I failed her, I failed her!"

We invited God to come into this place in her heart where all that pain had been stored. The Lord Jesus was able to come in as we prayed, and Jane was able to see the truth and let go of what psychology would call her "cognitive distortion" and what the Bible would call "the lie"—the deception that was the source of her pain. It was certainly not Jane's fault, but this was her childhood interpretation of what happened, and it had led to shame and a deep self-hatred. All of this had operated at a heart level, hidden and buried many layers deep. Most of our negative feelings have an inaccurate interpretation behind them, and when we change our interpretation of the event the pain often goes away.

Jane did not have to stay compulsively busy after that. She now realizes the benefit of the Scripture that says to "*be still, and know that I am God"* (Psalms 46:10 NKJV). She found peace and healing, but she needed to allow the pain to be exposed so the Healer could deal with it (Isaiah 53:5). Her healer that day was not me; it was not counseling or psychology that set her free from thirty years of shame and panic attacks. It was the truth spoken in a moment of prayer into a memory filled with misinterpretations. There isn't anything more fulfilling than seeing healings like this. There is nothing more exciting than to watch how the Lord Jesus brings true healing. I especially love the way each case is so unique. We have nothing to fear from a God who loves us like this, and He delights in setting us free even more than we are in being free!

Take a moment to inventory your addictions, asking God to expose the substances you have used and the more subtle addictions that you don't think about a whole lot. Beware of minimizing! Before stopping your physical addictions to substances especially, it is very important to get some help from your doctor. You may want to get a good counselor to walk you through the process too.

1. What addictions do you struggle with? Refer to and comment on all the substance addictions, but also the more subtle addictions that cause just as much harm.

_____

_____

_____

_____

2. Are there any ways that you are minimizing your addictions to yourself? Any areas of potential denial of your addictions?

_____

_____

_____

_____

Addictions

3. What do you use to self-medicate? What emotions might you be covering?

_____

_____

_____

_____

4. What are the main triggers that lead to your addictions?

_____

_____

_____

_____

5. Do without your addiction for a time today, or maybe all day, and journal as Jane did to allow yourself to see what you feel. What memories and pain came up in you when abstaining from your addictions?

_____

_____

_____

_____

ADDICTION A DEFENSE MECHANISM?

IT KEEPS YOU FROM WHAT YOUR FEELING

GOD IS OUR PROTECTOR, OUR DEFENSE
MECHANISM CAUSE US TO DROWN OR
ISOLATE

Chapter 9:
Compartmentalization

Compartmentalization refers to the way we process and think of the world around us. It is a defense mechanism, mostly cognitive, used to escape the difficult emotions that come with the complexity of having opposing thoughts and feelings in our hearts at the same time. Compartmentalizing in our thinking separates our world into different boxes or compartments to help us avoid the confusion, and the internal conflict, of having so many different values and competing emotional drives within us. This defense gets us to think out of one mindset exclusively, while avoiding the others. The compartmentalizer can then avoid and deny any perspectives that are outside of their "one-track mind" at that moment, which brings them a sort of false peace and comfort because their world is pretty cut and dried, or so they think at the moment.

Think of the multiple decisions you are making every moment and the value system that you have that processes these decisions every day. You love people, you love God, and you want to be honest. You want to serve and be kind to others, but you also want to take care of yourself. You also want to take care of your family and your friends. Think of the moral dilemmas that you face when you have to choose one over the other and determine how to handle the conflicts that result internally. Think back to our example out of the book of Hosea, and you will see a divided, compartmentalized heart in Gomer that needed to justify her decision-making. She had to simplify the internal chaos she had from having two lovers. She loved them one at a time, leaving one and embracing the other. She boxed her feelings for one up, closed the lid, and hid that part of her heart even from herself to allow for an easy and smooth transition when she went from one lover to the other.

Compartmentalizing is a cognitive function, and as many of our defense mechanisms run, it is a way to avoid the heart by living in the head. Having a compartmentalized view of your world will shelter you from feeling the confusion that gray areas bring. Black and white perspectives are so much easier to handle. However, in the end compartmentalizing will lead you to trade all that is in your heart for a cold and absolute existence, defined by some isolated compartment of your mind. Outside of the compartments of your thinking, you will have to admit that you are confused and conflicted and that you don't know what to do or how to think at times. Outside of your compartments you will be humbled, but inside them you feel as though you have it all together. The Bible says that we are like sheep. Sheep are, I am told, one of the stupidest animals on the face of the earth. This may be offensive to you and may raise some defenses in you (good time to check!), but not having to understand everything all the time is really quite peaceful. Compartmentalizers don't often appear humble and don't often deal with their hearts and their emotions. They're cut-and-dried decision makers who bypass the emotional pushes and pulls with others that are meant to build intimacy and bring us closer together.

Compartmentalization, like other defense mechanisms, is God given and extremely useful when used at the right time. Consider military personnel. They're taught early in training how to follow orders without thinking or feeling. Thank God they learn this so they can react quickly and safely. They are faced with opposing feelings and thoughts, such as the value of preserving human life versus their sense of protecting themselves or dealing with the urge to run versus completing their mission. They will often compartmentalize all other feelings and thoughts that would confuse their mission or stop them from standing firm as ordered. Their primary focus is following orders, and all opposing

Compartmentalization

feelings and thoughts are separated from their consciousness and not regarded. Because of this process, they get the job done. However, the box of opposing emotions and thoughts gets full and at some point and will overflow like a closet stuffed to the ceiling.

There are many other examples of how compartmentalizing is useful and needed at times. Teachers have to teach one concept at a time before presenting the complexities of language and math and science together. If you are a teacher, you probably compartmentalize a lot. You have to do this to teach successfully! However, emotionally and relationally these compartments we create to defend our hearts are not good for our well-being and need to be considered and prayed over. The bottom line is that you need to become aware of when you are using this defense.

Compartmentalization is often rewarded in our culture because those who use it are very productive. This is validated even if they are steamrolling over the needs and desires of others. "I'm busy right now," and "I can't think about that right now" are common thoughts of a compartmentalizer. They need to learn how to multitask and be sensitive to those around them. We can be vulnerable and share that we are overwhelmed and deal with the root emotions behind this defense, and we can feel the array of positive and negative feelings that are streaming through our hearts at any given minute—all at the same time!

The one-track thinking that we use in compartmentalization allows a simplification of understanding the world around us too, and thus falsely frees us from any emotion, any pain, any confusion, or any responsibility that lies outside of that single compartment from which you are thinking at that time. Because we, rather than God, tend to be in control of the compartments that we process, we will often choose compartments that block out what we do not want to see—we choose those that ease our pain and feed our egos. Religious training is a good example of this. It often leads people to look at how others are not following legalistic formulas and traditions, but self-righteously places themselves in the righteous compartment, therefore deceiving themselves.

The Journey into the Divided Heart

Compartmentalization can also be very self-serving. We are taught these formulas, these quick fixes for everything under the sun, using clichés in our speech and denying the complexity of our emotions and the diversity of the issues we share. It is a messy affair when we dive into our hearts! When we escape our compartmentalized thinking, God is often loosed to show us the areas of our hearts that are not peaceful and need healing. Seemingly without purpose and without your understanding of what He is doing, God may direct you to unpack all of the compartments of your heart. As He does this, you will feel overwhelmed, but you will also learn to give up the control that you are using to keep every thought and feeling in its proper place and order inside of you. The result? You will find true peace and, most importantly, allow yourself to be right in the center of God's will for your life. His direction will lead you instead of your own. His voice will be clear as a bell. How's that for a cliché?

Here are a few examples of self-serving, compartmentalized thinking that avoids pain and responsibility:

- A pastor leaves the church in conflict, but focuses only on this thought: "The Lord is calling me elsewhere."

- The grieving parent or spouse who says, "He is in a better place," to avoid the sadness, tears, and anger that they feel.

- The person who screwed up in one way or another who says, "That is all in the past," to avoid taking responsibility and learning from their mistakes.

- The boss who barks off orders because he is in charge, but compartmentalizes his relational side. He is giving up his friendships with those he is leading, thinking that his care and kindness will hinder his authority.

On a larger scale, we even compartmentalize our world into religious denominations. Because of this, we become culturally segregated, so we live and worship with those who are most like us, not those outside our compartments. Denominationalism, like compartmentalization, is simply a defense that we use to justify staying divided from each other

Compartmentalization

on a corporate and individual level. We feel we can stick others in a compartment or a box and never have to relate with them if their beliefs are different. Ethnic divides are another example of this. Alive and well, the seething hatred underlying much of the protesting and fighting we see in the news can only be compartmentalized for so long until the lid pops and violence ensues.

When we get outside of our compartments, there are not as many rights and wrongs, goods and bads, or blacks and whites as we wanted; in the real world, opposites of all kinds can exist at the same time, without us having to understand or be in control! The challenge from God is to be humble, to just be a stupid sheep and not try to hide the contrasts of every day's decision making. Instead, we should accept that we need daily discernment and guidance from above. You can get to a point where you can tolerate not wrapping your brain around everything in your world and not having a compartment for every opinion and emotion. You can eventually acknowledge that your own motives can be both good and bad at the same time. And you can eventually admit that some of what you do right is done for the wrong reasons, and some of what you do wrong is for the right reason. You can just put it out there and be a complex, emotional human, in a complicated and gray world, who needs a God to navigate the difficulties of everyday life!

A compartmentalized thinker feels confident about much of what he believes and does, but deep down inside he is just afraid of things feeling out of control when he does not understand something. To have an understanding in an area of life grants one control over it. This is why the Bible is so clear that we are not to lean on our own understanding, but acknowledge God, and from this place He can direct our paths (Proverbs 3:4-6). It is in this place of giving up our own understanding and our compartments that we can allow ourselves to feel the confusion, the pain, and the fear of uncertainty and be led *"in the way everlasting"* (Psalm 139:24 NKJV) as David called it.

Take a moment, take a step back, look at this defense of compartmentalization, and journal some about how it operates in you.

The Journey into the Divided Heart

1. Are you a black-and-white thinker in any area? How do you use compartmentalization to falsely simplify your life's circumstances?

_____

_____

_____

_____

2. Who are some of the people you tend to hurt the most when you get overly fixated on one thought or task and become insensitive?

_____

_____

_____

_____

3. How do you avoid your heart by staying compartmentalized in your head? Ask God to help you see at least one example of when you have done this.

_____

_____

_____

_____

4. What kinds of formulas and clichés do you use on yourself and others to "fix" problems? What would it be like to just be a stupid sheep with no real answers or easy solutions to dole out to others?

_____

_____

_____

_____

Chapter 10: Compensating

I love teaching about compensating because I have used this and have felt great relief when I put it at the foot of the cross. A compensator counterbalances their perceived weaknesses by emphasizing their strengths in other areas. They work harder in one area to excel and "compensate" for what they perceive to be their weaknesses in other areas of their life. A fragile ego or an overactive conscience (1 Corinthians 10:28-29) is prone to this defense mechanism because he cannot tolerate the pain of having weaknesses or wrongs. *"For all have sinned and fall short of the glory of God"* (Romans 3:23 NKJV). Instead of having peace and self-acceptance for their faults and weaknesses, the compensator will try to hide them by accentuating their strengths. They will not just accentuate their strengths verbally, but will strive to act out their perceived strengths in order to show the world and themselves that they are a worthwhile human being. Behind this defense mechanism we see that the overachiever and the driven people, are often the ones who are the most insecure on the inside. They compete all the time; winning is a must because their fragile ego fears feeling anything negative. A low self-esteem is underlying all this. Life is a competition, and other defenses like anger and isolation result when they do not win.

It is quite common for them to have had a past in which they were judged, rejected, or accused. Because of these wounds, they are trying their best to prove their accusers wrong. He or she is often fighting their past demons, past verbal curses, and arguing almost with themselves that they are right, even when no one is saying that they are wrong. The adult who was always told that "you will never amount to anything" is now trying to prove to himself and to others that this is not true.

The workplace and the home are common compensating environments. The worker who was fired or disciplined at their prior job will often now try to control and overachieve so much at their new job that they create chaos, shoving people out of the way while they try to prove that they are worth their position. The insecure and "shy" worker who always makes sure that they are too busy to talk when others are around is another example. Bosses can become controlling in their misguided effort to prove their worth, and workers often feel they have to hide their mistakes, protecting themselves from what they feel would be certain discipline. Perfectionists are often trying to compensate, and so are parents when they allow their kids to break all of the rules and spoil them because they have some idea that this will make up for bad things that happened to them.

Friends and significant others often compensate and hide their true heart from each other when they refuse to take risks in doing activities in which they think they may fail. These people may come across as shallow and "not fun," but really they are just afraid of being laughed at, which makes them avoid and compensate by focusing only on activities in which they think they will excel. Compensating takes the fun out of life and sucks the life out of you! It is allowing your defenses to focus you on perceived weaknesses and never doing anything out of joy or love, but constantly proving yourself instead, which in most cases never does truly work.

The root of compensating will always be the same. At some level, there is insecurity or hurt or an emotional wound that is being covered up by focusing on our strengths, striving in that area to cover what we think is our weakness. This is not God's way of dealing with our heart. He wants us to become strong by being weak (2 Corinthians 12:9) and by bringing all our weaknesses into the light (John 3). We do not have to hide our weaknesses or avoid them, but we do need to be mindful of using our strengths to cover them. We can practice and grow personally in these areas when we quit hiding our weaknesses (or what we think

Compensating

to be our weaknesses). How about being OK with the weaknesses you have and celebrating your shortcomings? How about laying down your need to prove to yourself and others by striving and working so hard? How about giving up the bitterness that feeds this defense mechanism and coming into the truth that you have made mistakes and that nothing can make up for them except asking for God's forgiveness through His Son Jesus? What instant relief you could feel by giving up this defense mechanism and just deciding to be yourself today!

Take a moment and journal out how this defense mechanism is being used to protect your heart.

1. What are your areas of weakness that you might try to cover with compensating?

_____

_____

_____

_____

2. What strengths might you use to cover your weaknesses?

_____

_____

_____

_____

3. How might you recognize striving in yourself? What areas would your loved ones say that you strive too hard in?

_____

_____

_____

_____

4. Have you had times of experiencing rejection? Journal the times you have felt this way, and ask Jesus to show you how to accept yourself with all your strengths and weaknesses.

_____

_____

_____

_____

Chapter 11: Denial

As they say, "de-nial is not just a river in Egypt," it is a defense mechanism, and it's one of the most primitive, but deadly, of the bunch. The Bible says that we will be *"ever seeing but never perceiving"* and *"ever hearing but never understanding"* (Mark 4:12); this is what denial tends to do to us. No matter how much the truth speaks to us about a matter, we are able to block it out like an ostrich who buries its head in the sand. Many of us do this by simply pretending a problem does not exist. We pretend our finances are OK when we cannot pay the bills, pretend our marriages are healthy when we really haven't been close for years, and pretend we are not mad at God when trauma visits our lives. These are all manifestations of denial. Denial is a spiritual problem; above all else, it is a form of psychosis (crazy thinking!) that we choose. This delusional thinking covers and avoids the pain in our hearts. I know that sounds intense, but I use the words *psychotic* and *delusional* on purpose because we have to wake up to just how crazy denial is. That is how hard this defense mechanism is to break through at times!

My son Ryan was nine years old and having an extreme reaction to a medication. My wife and I rushed him to the emergency room. While in the small triage area, our nurses brought in a cart full of what seemed like a hundred needles (exaggeration is also a common defense mechanism), and walked toward my son. They were preparing him for a blood draw, an IV, an anti-nausea shot, and who knows what else! I am not a huge fan of needles. (OK, you caught me minimizing and using sarcasm to cover my pain—both defenses.) In truth, I'm a major wimp when it comes to seeing blood and everything involved with it, but I wanted to be strong and take care of my son in his time of need, so when they began to notice that I was turning different shades of white, they asked, "Are you OK, Mr. Fair?"

What do you think I answered? I said, "I am just fine, thank you very much," hoping to get their attention off me as quickly as I could. My wife will tell you (without much prompting at all) that I was in "major denial" at that moment, and despite my best use of this defense mechanism I ended up in the room next to him down on a gurney, having almost passed out, sipping orange juice. Embarrassing? Yes! Did denial work? Not for a minute! My denial did nothing to relieve my problem.

Denial can be used for seemingly good motives like mine—I wanted to be there for my son, but nonetheless I was not making the best decisions when I denied the truth to try to hide the intensity of what I felt. Denial keeps us from admitting, even to ourselves, the reality of a situation when it seems too much for us to handle. Jesus came to make the blind see and we know that God says His people perish for lack of vision (Proverbs 29:18 KJV). Could it be that we are perishing in our disorders and problems, not because we are physically blind but because we are using denial unconsciously to cover the realities that are behind our difficulties? We are blind to what is happening in our hearts because we choose to live in denial of the unresolved issues that haunt us.

What does it feel like to realize that thousands go hungry each day while we spend money frivolously and take what we have for granted? What does it feel like to think of the reality of hell and an eternity (never-ending, ever) in torment separated from all that is good? What does it feel like to think that you could lose everything in a moment's time through any number of disasters and crises? Just talking about these realities automatically activates defense mechanisms we use to help numb our emotions and protect our hearts. These defenses are the delusions we use to avoid the tough issues of our world. Every day and every moment, there are triggers that overwhelm and threaten us. Denial, in any of its many forms, is often the first line of defense that we use to shelter us from the confusion, fear, anger, panic, and depression.

Denial

It is time to choose to open your eyes, listen to the voices of reason around you, and take a hard, but honest, look at what is going on in your life. Things may look great in some areas, but likely there are other areas in which you have not been honest with yourself. You have not been willing because you are too overwhelmed and scared to say, "Yes, I have a problem here."

Taking an honest look and opening your eyes to even the harshest of realities is often a relief, especially when the anticipation is that hardships will multiply from focusing on it. They don't. Maybe you have an addiction that you need to be honest with yourself about. Maybe you are having an affair and being unfaithful to your husband or wife. Maybe you have stolen and been dishonest with your boss. If you allow yourself to examine why you do these things, you may also decide to tell a chosen few what you have been hiding and *"confess your sins to one another"* (James 5:16 NASB). In so doing, you may lose a relationship, but maybe you won't. You may lose a job or even your freedom, but then again maybe you won't. We don't know the outcome! But I can promise that keeping yourself in denial (and hiding from others too) will always lead down a path of self-destruction because denial breeds further delusions in our thinking, which leads to worse and worse decision-making. Acceptance and accountability lead to proactive preventions that keep us from making similar mistakes. That is so much better.

Can you lay down your denial for a minute and look at the realities in your life and how you use this simple defense?

1. What areas in your life can you see that you have degrees of denial in?

_____

_____

_____

_____

The Journey into the Divided Heart

2. Who do you have in your life whom you would allow to confront your denial and listen to them? If no one, are you willing to begin letting someone into that role today?

_____

_____

_____

_____

3. What might your motives be for not wanting to see that which you are denying (fear, guilt, love)?

_____

_____

_____

_____

4. How would you feel if you found out that you really were not as good at your job as you thought, or your marriage was not as close as you thought, or you really do not have a relationship with God that is as close as you think?

_____

_____

_____

_____

Chapter 12: Displacement/ Projection

These defense mechanisms are ones that take some insight to overcome and are used much more frequently than we think. Even those who are trained to notice defense mechanisms don't recognize them easily. In essence, displacement is taking emotions that are related to interactions with one person or one set of situations and redirecting them to another relationship or another set of situations that feel safer and more tolerable. Displacement is not really just stuffing emotions, denying emotions, or distracting yourself from them; it is more of a "hot-potato" attempt to take what is uncomfortable and toss it at another person or thing to keep ourselves from getting burned!

Displacement is the act of taking emotions, wounds, and past traumas and "placing" them elsewhere, other than the place they originate. It works like this: if you get angry at your boss while at work, you may kick the cat when you get home and then yell at your wife. The cat and your wife are both safer places to vent your anger than the boss who has the power to fire you from your job. You take your anger about your boss and displace it, projecting it on others.

Another example of displacement can be seen in the child from a divorced family who acts like a perfect angel at the home of a parent who has been mostly absent, but gets home and directs all their anger toward the other parent who has been consistently home and caring for them. This is very confusing to the more consistent parent who expects to be treated better, not worse, than the absentee parent. Instead, that parent is considered the safer of the two and the child displaces their anger about the whole situation on the stable parent. Although this parent does have a reason to feel they are being treated unfairly, it helps them immensely when they find out that this displacement is happening because their child feels so safe and unconditionally loved by them!

When we place feelings like fear and rejection on others when they do not really feel that way, we are operating in displacement too. We are assuming they have these feelings based on how we feel. We may think another person is feeling rejected, unloved, or hurt, but in actual fact *we* are the ones really feeling those emotions! We can take any emotion and put it on someone else without even realizing it. We need to examine ourselves carefully to catch this very tricky defense mechanism.

Projections are very similar to displacement, but projection refers to the transference of thoughts instead of emotions. Just like a projector in the movie theater projects a film, we take a thought and transpose it onto the wall too. The film really isn't on the wall; it is back in the projector room, but it sure does look like it is on the screen. In the same way, our own thoughts sometimes look to us as if they belonged to other people. Projecting our own thoughts onto others is like a type of mind reading because we feel that we just "know" what another person is thinking or doing. These projected thoughts are based on our own confused thinking and help us buffer them by putting ownership of these thoughts on others. Many people feel rejected by others, but they are really projecting their own unresolved thoughts of rejection onto the people in their present day life. The sad thing is that the projection can become real because you act as though they have rejected you and in the process you reject them. An example is the husband who thinks his wife is cheating on him, but he is really reacting to his own internalized insecurities and jealousies that he will not admit to himself. He will push her away in the process.

The worst part about displacement and projection are that we are often guilty of judging others and then living in a state of near paranoia. That's what happens when we use this defense mechanism outside of

Displacement/Projection

God's direction and His truth. The Bible talks about discernment; it says we can realize what others are feeling and thinking by talking to them and by talking to God about it. God will often show you the thoughts you project and help you develop an ability to listen to Him above your own reasoning. He will show you this information, not to keep you from ever being hurt emotionally (that is part of living in a fallen world) but to help you understand and serve others around you. The judgments and conclusions we draw about others when we project and displace should not be tolerated by the believer. We are supposed to *"take captive every thought"* (2 Corinthians 10:5) and believe and speak the truth. It is damaging to ourselves and others when we form conclusions based on projected thoughts or respond with displaced feelings because they look or act similar to someone else who hurt us in the past. If we let them, these projections will lead us to trust no one. Even though our defenses will tell us we are safe, we will end up imprisoned in a type of solitary confinement. That's what happens if you embrace what this defense tells you to embrace.

These defenses are very important to understand as we work in the arena of prayer ministry and inner healing today. Most of us assume that whatever we were doing and whoever we were with when we became upset is the source of our pain. This could not be further from the truth. At Renewal Christian Counseling Center, we talk a lot about what triggers our feelings. Finding these triggers enables us to help people distinguish the triggers from the actual root of their pain. The reason we displace and blame so much instead of discovering the real root of our feelings is that it seems simpler and less painful to deal with them this way in the here and now. In contrast, getting insight into the real cause of our pain sounds daunting. When we continue to displace pain to present-day events and never get healing from the original bruise, that wound is never exposed and dealt with.

How many of us are not getting healed because it feels safer to focus on the triggers as the source of our pain instead of looking deeper at the wounds that have been there on our hearts figuratively for many, many years? It does take some confronting of your fears, thoughts, and emotions that you would swear are facts! There sure is a difference between fact and truth sometimes, and you may just find that some of your facts are a bit off and that the truth will set you free. It is not easy, but it is really worth it, as you then become free to heal, free to take ownership of your own emotions, and others are then free from the displacement and projections you put on them.

1. Can you think of a time when you used displacement or projection to minimize your own pain? Who did you displace your feelings on when you were triggered and upset?

_____

_____

_____

_____

2. Name one judgment that you have made recently that was really just a projection. Look at any feelings of rejection and anger at others, and see if there were really personal feelings that you did not own at the time.

_____

_____

_____

_____

3. What old wounds and bruises might you be projecting onto others in your life? These might be old traumas or areas of neglect. List them and get real with yourself.

_____

_____

_____

_____

Displacement/Projection

4. How would you know if you were projecting and displacing onto others? Would you be convicted by God? Do you have others who know you enough that they could see what was happening and would confront you in love? If not, who is one person you could pick to be an accountability partner to help you stop projecting onto others?

_____

_____

_____

_____

Chapter 13: Hopelessness

Hopelessness is usually described simply as an emotion, and it is. However, we often use one emotion as a defense mechanism against another to make life less painful and as a shield to cover the intensity of other underlying emotions. Hopelessness is one such emotion that we often use as a defense. A defense is anything used to avoid pain or buffer us from painful emotions. After experiencing the crash and burn of getting our hopes up and being disappointed over and over again, one solution is to simply not hope about anything ever again. This is simple enough, right? Hopelessness becomes a risk management tool used to minimize the occurrences of falling from the height of feeling hopeful about anything. Hopelessness is used to make sure we never let our dreams, our passions, or our faith lead to disappointment. It wards off that sense of feeling brokenhearted. Tragically, the areas where we have the most hopelessness are usually the areas of our hearts that once had the most hope. These hopes were perceived to have led to hurt and are now cut off by hopelessness, so the heart cannot be hurt by them again.

We feel that it is far safer to let the delusion of hopelessness become our reality than risk the falls we have experienced in the past. Do you remember being turned down when asking that girl or guy out on a date, and how next time it was easier just to think, "They would never say 'yes' to me so I won't even ask"? Do you remember rooting for that favorite sports team and after they have a losing season finding it hard to get excited and hope that they might make it happen this year

101

when the new season came? Do you remember almost getting out of debt? Has something always happened that pushed you backward again right about then? It was tempting to not even try any longer. We tend to accept the idea that "it will never happen, and I will just have debt for the rest of my life like everyone else. I better get used to it." Do you remember trying to trust someone after you had been hurt or even abused, and feeling that it was hopeless that anyone would ever treat you right, which justified going back into your shell?

Hopelessness is often connected to self-pity, and although it looks justified on the outside, don't be fooled. Someone could have a really rough past (could be you) and we should have compassion for them, but they can also be using hopelessness to justify and rationalize their own plan of self-protection. They are choosing hopelessness to protect themselves from the fear of failing and being let down in the future. Self-protection often leads to self-sabotage and leads the person to further justification of why there is no hope for particular areas of their lives. What a horrible cycle! This person seems to be stuck in their lives, their jobs, their lack of relationships, their finances, everything. Loving them is not feeling sorry for them, though; it is helping them to see that their own defense mechanisms are leading to their demise. Be prepared for denial, even anger, as they defend their right to hopelessness! The good news is that the abundant life God promises us in John 10 is on the other side of this defense and it is worth the risk!

Hopelessness is even more damaging when it is spiritually manifested. The believer "pursues" God with what they think is all their heart but never quite feels like they break through into a place of true relationship with Him. Instead of searching for defense mechanisms that may be shutting their heart down toward Him, it feels a whole lot easier to them to just take a stance of hopelessness, believing that they will never be as close to God as they would wish, or that God is just not that interested in them. The Word of God says:

> *"And now these three remain: faith, hope and love. But the greatest of these is love"* (1 Corinthians 13:13).

Hopelessness

Hope makes the top three, making this defense mechanism a definite blocker to the blessings God has for us! The Bible explicitly says that *"hope deferred makes the heart sick"* (Proverbs 13:12), so this defense mechanism can even lead to physical sickness.

It is time to take an inventory of any area in which you have shut down your passions, kept your heart from dreaming, and not allowed your spirit to see the hope that still remains. It may be scary to look at your hopes and dreams, and the voice of your defense mechanisms will certainly pipe up and tell you all kinds of reasons why you should not hope in these areas anymore. The voice of hopelessness will remind you of all the times that you hoped before and you did not get what you wanted. It will urge you to remember the foolishness of traveling down that road again and entertain you with the memories of disappointment, helplessness, and sadness you experienced before to warn you to avoid the letdowns increased expectations bring.

One simple definition of *hope* is "To desire of some good, accompanied with some expectation of it, or a belief that it is obtainable."[4] Hope is therefore connected to our desires and allows us to look forward. Hope is connected to our ability to believe, desire, and trust. Hope also helps us see, not just physically, but to "see," as the Bible says, with the *"eyes of your heart"* (Ephesians 1:18). Without hope you will not be able to see your ability to believe and trust—both primary pillars of healing and restoration. Hope is pretty important! A key misunderstanding that leads people to not hope is that they tend to judge their desires as wrong, self-centered, outside the will of God, or even as the source of their pain. People avoid hoping to protect themselves from hurt, but they also avoid hoping because they are afraid of sinning and being wrong and being the cause of their own pain! God wants to give us the desires of our hearts (Psalms 37:4). I challenge you to allow yourself to pursue your desires and hope again! Allow God to speak to your heart about your hopes and dreams again.

---

4. Websters Collegiate Dictionary, published 1910, s.v., "hope."

The Journey into the Divided Heart

God wants you to have your desires even more than you want you to have your desires! We are sometimes guilty of misunderstanding the true essence of what our desires are. We can also try to push that desire through in our own time and our own way. These are red flags to look out for, but hopelessness, shutting down, and repressing your desires is not the way that God would have us handle any facet of our hearts. Let's allow our heart's desires and hope and give up control of when and how these desires will come to pass. Let's also realize that the core hope behind many of our well-defined desires is really for companionship, joy, peace, and provision of basic needs. These are areas that God has promised to fulfill, but they may come in packages that we would not necessarily request or recognize.

1. What areas of your life do you have hopelessness about?

_____

_____

_____

_____

2. In what areas have you shut down your passions and dreams?

_____

_____

_____

_____

3. What areas are you willing to let your heart hope in again?

_____

_____

_____

_____

4. What desires have you judged to be wrong and why?

_____

_____

_____

_____

Chapter 14: Intellectualization

Avoiding your emotions and running away from your feelings by focusing on what you are thinking instead is called intellectualizing. Intellectualizing is when we rely on reasoning to avoid uncomfortable feelings, which makes it another form of emotional avoidance. Facts, statistics, analysis, and problem solving are all cognitive functions that serve as great diversions from our emotions. This particular defense mechanism is used and accepted in our society because intelligence is highly valued and its use is positively reinforced.

Neurologically, intellectualizing is using your left brain while avoiding your right brain. When we use this defense mechanism we rely on our intellect to buffer us from our right-brain emotions. Left-brainers are said to be logical thinkers. Right-brainers are considered emotional, passionate, adventurous, and creative. When we live life out of only our left brain, we lose who we really are, who we were created to be, and our passions, emotions, and relational capacity gets buried. Intellectuals sometimes feel like non-persons to others, as though they were robotic, sterile, and difficult to reach. There are payoffs to using this defense, though, or we would not use it so much. Not only do you not have to feel your negative emotions when intellectualizing, but you are positively reinforced by much of our culture for being smart, and you feel more in control.

Many were raised in households where one or both parents were very intellectual. They learned to value thinking and knowing facts as a measure of success and functionality. Some who use intellectualization don't know any other way to relate socially or handle the stress and emotions life throws at them. Some were raised in schools and churches that also taught them to intellectualize. Sometimes this happens just by modeling the importance of knowing more while ascribing emotions as weak and unstable. We learn many of our defenses from those around us, and like other defenses, many of us probably think our tendency toward intellectualization is part of our personality. Maybe you are more of a left-brainer. Avoiding emotion in your case shows that this is a learned behavior and a defense mechanism and not part of your personality.

In watching a sci-fi movie many years ago, there was a robot who looked and acted almost completely human. He helped the captain of a spaceship and has extreme intelligence, but always wishes that he had the ability to feel. Later in the plot, this robot is given a chip for his computer that allows him to feel emotions like a human. In one scene, the robot is transported with the captain to a horrible battle on the enemy's ship. Upon seeing this terrible enemy, he tells the captain that he is experiencing anxiety and that it is an intriguing sensation. The captain recommends that the robot turn off his emotion chip, at the same time expressing that sometimes he really envies the robot for having the ability to turn off those anxious emotions.

That is, in a sense, what we are doing when we turn to intellectualization. The emotions we feel are overwhelming at some point in our life, so our defense is to try to turn them off and become robotic. We don't necessarily have an emotion chip, though our right prefrontal lobe is dedicated to processing emotions, but we try to turn off our emotions much like the robot did by living in a purely intellectual state. This may be useful at times as it was for the robot in the movie; however, it becomes a default mode of operating when it goes unchecked, leaving our God-given hearts, passions, and feelings separate from our true person.

I have learned, and many of you have also, that *my* understanding is *not* to be trusted! Just when I think I know something or I understand something, I find out how little I really do know. It is not that my thinking isn't logical or factual, but it is so skewed by my own experiences, my own prejudices and short-sightedness, that is not to be trusted alone. If

Intellectualization

you haven't had the thought that you just wish you could flip a switch and turn your own brain off, if you haven't thought that a lobotomy sounded pretty good some days, then you haven't caught on to how damaging this defense really is. You haven't learned to *"lean not on your own understanding"* (Proverbs 3:5). I guess you could say that it is time that we all got out of our minds and into our hearts! If you feel like a robot, if you are a gatherer of meaningless facts, if you find yourself debating instead of relating with others, you are likely using this defense.

Rationalizing, justifying, debating, and racing thoughts are all forms of intellectualizing. Rationalizing is used to justify bad behavior and decision-making and to cover mistakes with reasoning that the person often knows is just an excuse. We use it to defend ourselves from emotional attacks and from having to feel; instead, we use our intellect to argue. Really, when it comes down to it, this defense mechanism is an intellectual way to avoid taking responsibility. When we don't take responsibility for our actions, we can't learn and grow, and relating with others becomes pretty difficult. Rationalizing our behaviors and decision-making is impersonal and superficial and prevents both people in a conversation from entering into any real heart-to-heart interaction.

Debating can be an offshoot of rationalizing, and it usually uses intellectualizations as part of its arsenal. The goal of debating is to show oneself as right and others as wrong. It is really a form of fighting. It does not resolve conflict and often leads to its participants being further at odds with one another than they were before the debate. We can unite and reconcile and have intimacy of the heart, but our heads, with all their intellectual tendencies to debate, will very seldom find true togetherness in their interactions.

Many of us struggle with racing thoughts at times too, which is more of an unconscious means of intellectualizing. Nevertheless, it is thinking at a very fast pace with the same goal of controlling emotions by problem solving in our heads. The best example I have heard of this was a client who told me that her racing thoughts were like watching a train go by, with each box car being a thought. She said, "I just begin to focus in on one train car before it passes out of sight. The next cars come into focus, but they also pass out of sight before I can really see them." She was describing the pace of her thoughts and the frustration of trying to focus on one while it was constantly being replaced by a stream of more and more worrisome thoughts. Isn't that how it feels when we have racing thoughts? The thoughts in our minds manifest way too fast when our intellectualizing and planning gets out of control. We find no true peace in this defense. Racing thoughts are just a manifestation of the intellect revving up its RPMs to high gear when fear is injected into the mind. Like a car that is driven hard, this defense mechanism will destroy the body and unfortunately brings physical pain and diseases with it like fibromyalgia, chronic fatigue syndrome, TMJ, restless leg syndrome, and hypertension among others. Click into your right brain and emotions when this is happening, journal some and your heart will not need to activate this defense as intensely.

In America, knowledge is often our god. We have learned to lean on our own understanding to feel in control. We are told in the Scripture to:

> *"Trust in the Lord with all your heart and lean not on your own understanding; in all your ways acknowledge him, and he will make your paths straight"* (Proverbs 3:5-6).

This is one of my favorite Scriptures, and a very convicting one for those who need to understand everything, who need to think everything out, and who feel in control only when they can intellectualize the world around them. This is telling us that God's way is just the opposite. This leaves us feeling vulnerable, defenseless at times, and out of control, which is the perfect place to actually learn to trust in Him. We somehow feel that we have the right to understand everything God is doing, as if we could comprehend His explanation even if He told us. His ways are higher than our ways (Isaiah 55:9), and God calls us to give up everything we know to follow Him and to get the healing we need. He truly will "direct our paths" if we will learn to submit to Him.

There isn't a deadlier set of defenses than these; they have grave spiritual effects. There is a lot of pride operating in intellectualizing. Jesus speaks about giving up our pride in John 3 (among other places). This chapter explains the whole concept of being "born again." He gives us a picture of what being born again actually means and how to know if we have really taken this step in our lives. He says in John 3:3 that *"no one can see the kingdom of God"* unless he is born again. John 3:8 says that when you are born again you are like the wind and don't know where you are coming from or where you are going.

Wow! Just think about that for a minute! You do not know where you are coming from or where you are going! How would that feel to you to live every day without a clue as to where you had been and where you were going? You would not be able to look to your past for your future. You wouldn't know what you were doing next. You would have no understanding of what your plans were and why and how to avoid the mistakes of your past. Nicodemus was struggling with this when he said, "Must I enter my mother's womb a second time?" referring to being born again (John 3:4). Nicodemus was looking at the scope of going back to a place where he knew *nothing*, where he understood *nothing*, and where his mind was not filled with his dependence on his own intellect (which works so forcefully against our faith). For we *"walk by faith, not by sight"* (2 Corinthians 5:7 NKJV). Our physical eyesight and our intellectual eyesight work together to sustain our sense of control. Jesus was saying that salvation was all about giving up our intellectual control to Him.

Some will answer, "Well, God gave us a brain so that we can use it!" and "It is not good stewardship to not plan ahead," but these are the words of Jesus here, not mine. Again, John 3:8 says *you do not know where you are going!* Jesus understood that our motives for planning and thinking ahead are often based on fear; they require little faith because they get us to depend on *ourselves,* not God. In addition, we truly do not know our future, so how can we plan for it in the first place? God alone knows which way He wants us to go. Only in trusting Him and following His lead will we find that path. If we go our own way, we could easily miss the destiny He has for us.

Defenses like these are often used not only internally to deal with our emotions but are verbalized in a way that triggers others into feeling belittled and patronized. Intellectualizing is certainly one of the defenses that causes pain in others. As we protect ourselves out of self-centeredness and focus on the facts of any given situation, we also become insensitive to what others are feeling, what they need, and how our words are affecting them. We need to learn to stay away from this defense. Scripture says:

> *"Be not wise in thine own eyes: fear the Lord, and depart from evil"* (Proverbs 3:7 KJV).

1. What do you feel like when you are intellectualizing? Are you aware of your emotions at all? When do you think you learned to intellectualize?

_____

_____

_____

_____

2. Do you ever have racing thoughts, debate with others, or base your esteem on your facts and opinions? Name a time you remember when you had racing thoughts. Name a time when you used rationalization to cover your tracks. Name a time when you used debating to protect yourself. Journal about these instances.

_____

_____

_____

_____

_____

_____

Intellectualization

3. Are you born again? How do you know that you are? Do you live a life of being like the wind and "knowing not where you come from or where you will be going"?

_____

_____

_____

_____

4. Are you willing to give up the pride of leaning on your own intellect and understanding if it is hurting you, those around you, and separating you from God? This is a great time to humble yourself and pray.

_____

_____

_____

_____

Chapter 15: Minimizing

Minimizing is one of the easiest defense mechanisms to catch because of the common phrases that come with it. It can be a very subtle defense. It's all about a person lying to themselves and others by covering painful truths. Yes, minimizing is lying! That's sounds like a strong statement, but it is true. Many times we are not even aware that we are minimizing and wouldn't recognize that we are lying. Why? Minimizing has a component of denial to it that covers the truth by subtly skewing the severity and intensity of the subject at hand. It is one of the key defense mechanisms we use to turn a blind eye toward what we know about right and wrong too, and it can deceive us into believing that there are little to no consequences related to our actions. Minimizing statements include: "I didn't really do anything wrong," or, "It really wasn't that bad." These statements keep us from taking full responsibility for our actions. If we do not see the severity and the damage that our thoughts and behaviors are causing others, then we feel we have no reason to repent and change.

There is a classic fable that many of us have heard throughout the years about a gossip who minimizes the effects of the rumor that was spread. She is later confronted on her actions by a wise man of God in her life. When confronted she says, "I only told one or two friends" (only is a key word in minimizing). The wise man asks her to bring him a feather pillow, takes her to a high place, and has her cut the pillow open so the feathers are scattered and blown in the wind. The wise man of God then says to her, "Now, will you please retrieve all the feathers and replace them back into the pillow." She answers that the task would be impossible. She is then told, "So it is with your slanderous words that have been spread." Only then is she able to see the fuller effects of gossip having been spread abroad like the feathers in the wind; that there is no way to ever take them back. Her minimizing was confronted and the true effects of her actions revealed.

Much of what we think is "no big deal" really is a big deal. We don't want to look at our mistakes for what they really are, usually because we already feel condemned and ashamed. Our self-protection and defense mechanisms are used to keep us from feeling shame and disappointment with ourselves about our mistakes. If we were to get past this type of defense mechanism and not fall into condemnation, then we could see our behaviors, our "stinking thinking," our anger, and our issues, and use these revelations to make decisions to *change* for the better. Minimizing robs us of those choices. We need to see ourselves accurately. If we can create an atmosphere of mercy, grace, and safety in making mistakes, then those around us can stop minimizing their mistakes too. We could all take responsibility without shame and grow as a result.

Addictions often include minimizing as a way to contain the denial system that makes us feel that "everything is good" and "everything is OK." A drinker may say that "I just had a little to drink" or "I only had a few." Minimizers will describe their drinking behaviors as "occasional" and "once in a while." They will say, "It really doesn't hurt anyone when I drink," when the drinking is actually more severe than they wish to admit. Minimizing uses the tongue to try to make a molehill out of a mountain instead of the other way around. The goal is to water down the problem enough so that change is unnecessary. Being confronted by others is the only real hope that we have to escape this false reality, which is why treatment programs are so important. We just can't see past this defense mechanism by ourselves once it is firmly in place. If others like our sponsor or accountability partners are saying we are out of balance, it may be time to take a good, hard, honest look at ourselves. It's time to repent (or change our minds) and give up our minimizing thoughts. We should not fear the way we really are.

Minimizing

Minimizing is not only used to cloak negative behaviors and addictions, it is used most often in dealing with our feelings and emotions in general. When asked about feelings that we label as wrong or bad, we may say that we are "just a little upset" when we are really angry or even in a rage. We may say we were "just a little bit frustrated" when we are super overwhelmed instead. We often say we are "having a bad day" or feeling "a little out of it" when we are really depressed. Likewise, fear is not fear; it is minimized into being "just a little tense" or having "a few worries on my mind." All of these false descriptions tend to protect us from the intensity of our emotions internally at the cost of us having minimal to no insight. Having insight could lead to us seeing where these emotions are coming from and then changing the thinking behind them, but minimizing makes this almost impossible. It is a real hindrance to positive change of any kind.

Most of us have been taught that we are supposed to be OK and haven't been taught that it is OK to not feel OK. We've been taught that it may be acceptable to have a little of this feeling or a little of that emotion, but it's not acceptable to express the fullness of what is going on inside of us when our emotions are intense. Sharing intense emotions should not be against our rules. Jesus had some pretty intense emotions. Have you ever thought of how intense His fear was when He sweat blood in the garden (Luke 22:44)? How about when He wept when His friend Lazarus died (John 11:35)? What about the righteous anger He displayed when He turned over the tables in the temple (Matthew 21:12)? If Jesus didn't minimize, then neither should you!

Be honest with yourself and those you love. Be respectful as you are sharing and use "I" statements rather than "you" statements (these are blaming statements), and share *about* the emotions you feel instead of sharing *from* them. You can do this without minimizing. It is OK to have negative feelings. It is normal and OK to express them honestly without letting ourselves act them out. All this covering up prevents us from receiving help and counsel from those who love us. Minimizing does us no favors. You will find a lot of freedom when you let go of this defense and get honest while being respectful.

The Journey into the Divided Heart

A simple tool to get around minimizing is to begin to identify your emotions and then rate them on a scale from one to ten, with ten as the most intense and one as the least. Then ask yourself what scale of emotional intensity you feel, but also ask a friend, spouse, or coworker to help you rate your emotions too. Chances are that their description will be more accurate than yours and will help you take a more honest look at what is happening in your heart. Their assessment will also help you see how much minimizing is going on in your life. This process will help you pursue the truth that will set you free. We must see reality. We must admit to the degree and intensity of the issues we face!

1. When was the last time that you minimized a mistake that you made? When was the last time you minimized an emotion?

_____

_____

_____

_____

2. If you were to recognize your mistakes in light of their actual intensity, what might you feel? What is the hardest part of realizing that you have made big mistakes?

_____

_____

_____

_____

3. What are the symptoms of your minimizing? In what areas are you most prone to using this defense—work, home, relationships, another area?

_____

_____

_____

4. Are you willing to begin rating your feelings and thoughts on the scale of intensity that they really are? Will you challenge your own ratings by allowing yourself an accountability partner to help you find any minimizing that may be operating?

_____

_____

_____

_____

Chapter 16: Regression

We all look foolish at times, especially when we are emotionally stirred up or "triggered." I've seen adult temper tantrums that have outdone the best three year olds! At the height of our emotions, we tend to look, and act, ridiculous; it can be a little embarrassing. What's even scarier is that we tend to think like a little kid too. Our logic is distorted, and our ability to take things in correctly gets skewed. It is as if we are seeing and understanding things at a grade school level. When we are emotionally activated and acting and thinking this way, we are in a state of "regression."

Regression is a return to a much earlier developmental stage. This happens when we are really emotional inside or having thoughts that we are trying to avoid. When we use this defense we do not act mature, we do not use our self-control, and we do not rely on our reasoning to help us. It is as if they had all gone to lunch! Regression is quite common and, like many other defense mechanisms, operates on a completely subconscious level. We get mad and yell; we get hurt and pout; we feel rejected and withdraw. In clinical situations, we commonly see regression in a traumatized teen sucking his thumb or wetting the bed. We see traumatized adults who cannot sleep alone anymore or need the lights on at night because of their fear. Any developmental milestone is at stake when regression has its way. It is not uncommon for those who have gone through severe trauma to have to relearn how to care for themselves—this includes hygiene, cooking, eating, and handling their finances.

The Journey into the Divided Heart

When emotionally triggered, some people regress back to places in their development when they were traumatized in their past. They may be fifty and regress back to hiding in a closet like they did when they were abused as a kid. Divorces can cause people to regress to the time when they were first separated from their parent. Others may regress back to a time when they were a student or when they were rejected or picked on as a child. Many of us simply shut down when angry, hurt, or embarrassed (primitive avoidance defense), run away (flight response), or just snap back in anger (fight response), but some will go back much further and to much more infantile behaviors such as soothing themselves by rubbing their arms, rocking, or through sucking a thumb, finger, etc.

Regression can be very subtle or it can be blatant, but either way this defense has us looking and acting like a child when we are hurt and in emotional pain. Paul said in the New Testament:

> *"When I was a child, I spoke as a child, I understood as a child, I thought as a child; but when I became a man, I put away childish things"* (1 Corinthians 13:11 NKJV).

It is time to put childish ways behind us. The next time a friend does not call you back, it doesn't mean that she does not like you. Next time someone is having a bad day and barks at you in a hurtful way, you may feel scared or hurt, but you do not have to retaliate. Adults may tend toward the equivalent of sticking out our tongues, crossing our arms, turning our heads, kicking and screaming, and regressing to thinking like a toddler when we are upset, but it does not have to go this way. Let's leave this behind, and when we are tempted to regress realize that our heart is hurting and responding with this defense to attempt to contain the pain that it is feeling. When you notice regression is starting or you are in the middle of it, this is a good time to look behind it. Look into your heart and find out what you are really feeling and what memories are surfacing. It's likely that some trauma from that time period is surfacing. Why? Because it needs healing! Making a conscious decision to give up regression and seek healing from trauma will bring you the peace you deserve.

Regression

1. When you act younger than your age, what types of behaviors do you notice?

_____

_____

_____

_____

2. Do any of your regressed behaviors remind you of being very young? What age would you ascribe to your regressive behaviors?

_____

_____

_____

_____

3. Do you have any subtle self-soothing types of behaviors? Rocking, rubbing, holding objects of affection when you are really upset?

_____

_____

_____

_____

4. What triggers can lead to regression for you? What trauma might be triggered that would lead to this defense mechanism?

_____

_____

_____

_____

Chapter 17: Repression/ Suppression

Repression is often just called stuffing. When we repress our feelings, we are stuffing them inside. I like to call stuffers *turkeys* because they're all full of stuffing. In order to understand repression further, let's compare our minds to a computer. A computer has two separate systems for memory. The hard drive is where we load software like the operating system and store long-term data and information. We push the save button and our computers store information deep inside on this specific component called the hard drive. We also have a type of memory called RAM (random access memory) that is used to access data more quickly, data that is needed on a moment by moment basis. RAM keeps programs or applications actively running so that we can access this information without having to retrieve it from the hard drive. You can think of *repression* as using our long-term memory, our hard drive, to protect our emotional selves. We shove and stuff our emotions from RAM memory to our long-term hard drives.

In contrast, *suppression* is when we use our short-term RAM to protect ourselves emotionally. When we suppress, we put our emotions and memories away in the back of our RAM in such a way that we are much more conscious of the memory and its related pain, but are distracting ourselves from feeling it. Similar to repression but much more powerful in its effects of making emotional pain more unconscious is disassociation (which we will study further in coming pages). *Dissociation* is when we remove ourselves even further from our emotions by "unplugging" from the hard drive and disconnecting from it altogether

When we repress memories and the feelings and thoughts that go along with them, we are essentially taking information and consciously filing it as deep as we can in the archives of our long-term memory in hopes that we will never find it again. We are choosing to forget, which is why repression is sometimes called "motivated forgetting"—it's our attempt to push thoughts and memories out of our consciousness. We can become very good at this process and our choosing to forget can move at the speed of light once we have adopted and used this defense mechanism regularly.

There was an old movie that I saw once where a man had fallen deeply in love with the woman of his dreams. She would have no part of him and he becomes depressed and brokenhearted. The man and his friend decide to join the army and leave for a far away land in an effort to forget her and his grief. So off they go, and intermittently in their trip, the one friend asked the other if he had forgotten the woman yet. But the question just serves to irritate the grieving man until he finally explodes on his friend to stop reminding him of her, saying that the questions were interfering with the forgetting process. But the annoying friend keeps asking anyway, making it impossible for him to repress his pain.

Like the brokenhearted man in this movie, we repress and try to forget the past because it is just too painful to handle. We don't want that painful information in our RAM where it is easily accessed because it would hurt too much if it was that close to the surface. Most people want to heal from their emotional trauma and pain, but many are not doing so because they don't know that we have a God who is able to heal every hurt and every wound in our lives. They know no other alternative but to repress it. They actively stuff their history and try to move on with life. A woman who was abused as a child might stuff her trauma feelings so deep that when asked, she will report that "it was nothing" and actually believe that herself. Why? Because that memory is not even loaded in her RAM. A man who hit his wife might consciously hide the details to protect himself, but he may also feel so guilty that he represses the memories deep enough that he can pretend to himself that he only just yelled at her (minimizing there too).

Have you ever thought about what your past really is? Have you thought that every second that is not the present is in your past? Have you ever thought that by the time you get done reading this sentence, that that moment is now in your past? Why do we work so hard to put the past behind us when it is an active part of our everyday lives? The past is all you have experienced before the microsecond that you are living in right now! Leaving all the past unresolved to influence the future is a dangerous thing. It takes a lot of denial to lead to repression, and many people think this how their lives should be run! They use the idea that they should put the past behind them to rationalize and justify their repression.

Many people, especially Christians because of theology they have been taught, think that we are supposed to leave the past in the past. They were taught to not "cry over spilled milk" and were told that "there is nothing you can do about the past, so just move on." Some were told that if they cry, "I will give you something to cry about" by their parents. They may have been theologically trained that they are a *"new creature"* and that *"old things are passed away; behold, all things are become new"* (2 Corinthians 5:17 KJV), so if one is *"in Christ"* their life should be one of only love, joy, and peace. This is an accurate statement describing our new life in Christ, but it does not mean we never have to deal with our old injuries and negative emotions; they do not simply disappear when we get saved. Because people feel they must, they repress any memory or feeling that does not feel positive in their effort to be the Christian they think they should be. These theologies, teachings, and directions are often taught early in our lives. They can also be taught simply through modeling and remain completely unspoken. When we are taught these ideas by our family, our churches, and our culture, we are actually being taught to use repression as if it were a good, godly, and healthy way to handle our emotions. The sad thing is that this was learned from parents who learned from grandparents who learned from generations back in their history. This generational repression becomes a huge barrier to healing, counseling, and even to having heart-to-heart conversations with the people we love. Repression is not godly maturity; maturity of character is feeling your emotions and reacting only to Christ in the midst of them.

There is a time to just move on, move forward, and put things behind us, but this comes after we have sorted through the emotions, weeded out any perspectives that are leading to long term forgiveness and trust issues, and looked at it squarely in the eye. Reconciliation and forgiveness often come from taking an inventory and letting ourselves process past conflicts and our interpretations of them. We can change our future and redeem our past by changing the thinking we developed from these experiences. Our past is part of who we are and how we are choosing to live in the present. It can't be disconnected from who we are and how we behave without repression, but it can be used to bring good life lessons, understandings, and strong building blocks that are the foundation of character and wisdom once it is understood through God's eyes. When people think they are just leaving it all behind, they are really repressing and suppressing their past and need the help of a good counselor, pastor, and friends to sort through the data in their hard drive together. Then their future will be markedly different, and they will be able to walk in freedom in Christ.

Instead of "motivated forgetting," then, we can choose "motivated remembering" that is God-led. I don't want people digging for buried memories just for the sake of remembering trauma and pain in my office. This is not the means that leads to healthy change! However, our hearts remember and store what we need to know, and I desperately want all of us to live and operate from our hearts, allowing ourselves to listen to our heart when it is telling us we have some unresolved pain to work through in our past. The healing process often starts by simply allowing our heart to feel. When we do this, there are a lot of memories and related feelings that naturally spring forward. When we consciously stop repressing and allow ourselves the natural process of feeling our emotions, we can heal from our past. The purpose of counseling, or inner healing, then is so much deeper than just discovering what was repressed. True healing comes when these memories have closure because we see them through God's eyes.

Freud and other psychoanalysts thought that most of our difficulties came from "repressed memories," which meant to them that the goal of therapy was to find and change hidden memories to work through their influence in our lives. Freud thought that through dream analysis, interpretation of family dynamics, looking at our slips of the tongue ("Freudian slips"), and recovery of consciousness of the past, we could heal the present. Much of psychotherapy today is caught up in this modality of treatment, which can be very dangerous and lead a person to deeper oppression than they had before starting these treatments. Repression is indeed a true defense mechanism that needs to be addressed, but once it is removed, our goal in therapy is to help change a person's thinking through the power of God! The thinking that needs to be changed though is often hidden behind repression. Consider what God says about how change happens in Romans 12:2:

"Do not conform any longer to the pattern of this world, but be transformed by the renewing of your mind. Then you will be able to test and approve what God's will is—his good, pleasing and perfect will."

This means that we are transformed or changed by not just understanding what's in our subconscious, but rather by "renewing" our minds. The Bible says that we can have *"the mind of Christ"* (1 Corinthians 2:16) and we can think the way that He thinks! We can walk through all those repressed memories and weed out the shame, the anger, the fear, and the vows we have made to never trust again. We can walk through those memories with others and learn a different way to cope with the emotions that came with them. Like one of my clients said so accurately, "Looking back now after therapy, I can see that all the negative emotions and memories in me that I was stuffing down were really like a huge beach ball that I was always constantly having to balance on top of to push down in the water. It was the repressing of this all in itself that was depressing me more than the beach ball of memories and feelings themselves." What a job it is to contain all that is inside us—seeing these old feelings and wounds leaking out into our present-day lives, but stuffing them in the back of our memory because we were taught that this is the right way to cope.

If you would take a minute right now to just let that beach ball surface, you may get some important revelations in your life. If you would take a moment to give up repression and look at the present day issues in your life, you will find there are specific feelings and memories that have led to your present perspectives and reactions. This could be the day we start to walk through it together. Some of you will see that repression is becoming too tiring, that your inner emotional closet is full and you cannot stuff any more inside. You can find relief today by releasing your emotions, relaxing, and letting your heart send any unresolved information up to you from the hard drive inside. Let yourself grieve and get closure and the healing that you deserve.

1. Revisit at least one difficult memory in your past, and see how deep you have to dig to access it. Does finding this memory and its emotions seem more like accessing the RAM of your computer (easy and fast), the hard drive of your computer (buried a bit and saved deep in the archives), or like it is dissociated (as though you are totally disconnected from the computer drive it is stored on)?

_____

_____

_____

_____

2. What do you do to help repress emotions, and how do you get your emotions to stay repressed? Hint: distracting yourself, self-talk, etc.

_____

_____

_____

_____

3. What were you taught about how to handle emotions? Were you told not to cry, or maybe even taught spiritually that we are to leave the past in the past without walking through the emotions? If so, stop and look at what you believe and if you were actually being taught to use repression.

_____

_____

_____

_____

4. What would it be like if all the memories of your life, good and bad, were downloaded from your long-term hard drive memory to your RAM inside? What memories and traumas do you think would be the most painful to have in your conscious memory? Are you willing to walk through these with others who care for you deeply so you are healed?

_____

_____

_____

_____

Chapter 18: Sublimation

Y ou've heard in the earlier days of heavy metal rock and roll that if you played certain songs backward you could hear a subliminal message. On the surface, you hear one message with a catchy tune, but when you play it backward you could hear the real message of the band that was "sublimated" and hidden beneath the surface. They call this backmasking. A subliminal message was embedded within the music beyond the conscious perception of the listener. This is similar to the way sublimation works as a defense mechanism.

Sublimation is often described as a method of channeling unwanted desires and impulses into smaller and less harmful means that are socially acceptable. Oftentimes we will act out our anxious feelings by cleaning the house, our aggressive feelings in over-disciplining our kids, and other socially acceptable actions to work out our negative emotions and urges. Much of sublimation is actually based on our perception of socially acceptable! For instance, rock music may be annoying to some, but not necessarily socially unacceptable. However, the subliminal message of hate, murder, and satanic propaganda that a few rock bands were spreading wasn't socially acceptable. So the band passed these ideas on subliminally through backmasking instead of saying them outright.

We channel our socially inappropriate impulses and intense feelings in a variety of ways. Most sublimation looks good and may even have lasting positive effects, but there is a motivation behind it that is begging for our attention. Sublimation helps us to curve and channel impulses that are not acceptable to us into acceptable means so that we can still feel good about ourselves and yet have an outlet to express what is really happening inside.

I remember not getting my way as a teenager. I was mad but did not know how to deal with my anger or how to just submit and trust in that moment. I went to my room, cranked some music really loud, and worked out as hard as I could. The passive-aggressive message I was sending was not all that subtle. The sublimation of channeling my anger into exercise instead of yelling was the defense I chose. I guess working out was a lot more appropriate than yelling or swearing at my parents, but there was still some junk for me to look at inside if I was to be really honest with myself.

How many of you have used working out or exercise to cope when you are angry and upset? I'm not trying to discourage exercise. I want to help you see that you are using a defense mechanism and avoiding your need to work through your anger. My subliminal message to my parents was that I was angry. I think they heard it loud and clear. It's likely that you have a lot of ways that you send messages subliminally too. I could have worked out that day and also worked through my anger appropriately. I needed to learn to resolve conflict, submit to authority, and have respectful conversations with others, which didn't necessarily happen because I used a defense mechanism to avoid and hide instead.

In order to look at how sublimation works in our lives, we have to be able to identify the drives in us that we feel are unacceptable socially and what channels we use to act them out. Take a moment and look at some of your internal impulses and see how you would define them to yourself. If you think something that you want or need is wrong, then you will not be able to express yourself in these areas and you will be conflicted as to how to handle your emotions. You will feel like a balloon that is going to burst, but you don't have a way to appropriately express what you feel. Or it could be the opposite. You may feel empty inside from a perceived need that you don't know how to get met appropriately, so you use a subliminal way to pursue your need.

134

Sublimation

A key area in which we find sublimation is in relationships, sexuality, and physical touch. God gave you a need to be touched. Some of you may project (already covered that one!) negativity onto touch because you have had bad experiences with touch in your past, but it is a necessary and God-given part of attachment, which will be explained later in the interventions section. Most people would say that touch is not wrong in itself, though we have to draw boundaries against inappropriate sexual and violent touch. Based on where and how you were raised, you learned a lot about physical touch—when to hug, when to kiss (you Italians know what I mean!), when and if to reach out to shake hands or hold the hand next to you. Touch is a basic need programmed into humans by God and there are volumes of books written in developmental psychology outlining that touch is not just a *want* but a *need*. Whole therapies have been devised around massage and the healing touch to address what some call "touch deprivation" and "skin hunger." Our society is one of the most distant in all the world with a personal space of two to four feet with strangers where the study of personal space (proxemics) will tell you that other cultures have an average distance of much, much less! But if this need is being unmet and you have no relationships in your life that you could appropriately get touch from, what do you do?

As you look at your personal space and your need for touch, let's look at what is acceptable for you and what is not. Is it acceptable for you to hug someone you know? Is it acceptable for you to hug someone you are just meeting? If the answer is "yes" to only very close friends, to dating relationships, and sexual relationships such as your husband or wife (though many of you have sadly given up touching even with your spouse!), then what are you to do if you do not have those kinds of relationships at this point in your life? These drives could be sublimated elsewhere because they are not easily suppressed for long periods, and you need an outlet. If some people could, they would simply get rid of any and all personal needs because they feel trapped and stuck with these needs. To alleviate the drives that you have would require disassociation, which is not at all healthy.

The Journey into the Divided Heart

What then do we do to sublimate our need, our drive, our desire for touch? We find alternatives that are labeled as acceptable in society. These acceptable means of receiving touch could be things like massages, seeing the hairdresser weekly, pets, blankets and dolls for kids. Many find a replacement for touch in hidden sexual behaviors such as sexual addictions to pornography as they often masturbate while watching porn, and some may even resort to sexual affairs and prostitution while the real internal motive is simply that they want to be touched.

The unmet need for touch is sublimated into our sexuality because our culture, though it has strict limits on personal space, has an overall acceptance and fixation on sex. Sex, though not bad and created by God to be enjoyed within the bounds of marriage, can actually become the main avenue to sublimate many unmet emotional needs, which explains why sexual addictions are so rampant in our culture. When using sex and sublimation though, the sad thing is that the person never really does get their true emotional needs met. Instead they enter the addiction cycle of needing more and more sexual activity to satisfy a valid unmet emotional need of which they are not even aware. On top of that, they then feel ashamed about what they are doing.

Even more complex is the subject of how marriages become a place of sublimation in which partners expect all their emotional needs to be met in the marriage. This puts unreal expectations and pressure on their marriage and threatens its survival. Some in this situation are living in denial of their needs for other friendships, support, touch, and intimacy (intimacy is not sex) outside of their spouse. We put our marriage on a pedestal and define it as an outlet for all our needs for physical touch. This codependent behavior is not healthy, even though it looks good, healthy, and even a protection from sexual sin. Instead, it is in itself leading to the demise of some marriages because we are putting an unhealthy expectation on our marriages alone. God created us to explore a diversity of relationships in our families, in our churches, and in our communities. We are sabotaging our marriages by trying to use them to sublimate all our needs for touch among other needs.

Sublimation

Other impulses and needs within us should also be explored. We have emotional impulses too—anger, loneliness, rejection. Many people divert anger into physical activity such as physical exercise, working out, running, etc. Others pour their feelings into their work. These activities have many benefits and lead to many positive effects; however, if the root cause of the sublimation is not found and addressed, you will feel a physical release of the anger, but the emotional and spiritual effects of that feeling will remain present internally. The Bible says, *"Don't let the sun go down while you are still angry, for anger gives a foothold to the devil"* (Ephesians 4:26 NLT). Sublimating anger and channeling it in other directions will not restore the angry heart to a place of redemption and reconciliation to others; it will only serve to distract and repress it.

Lonely feelings are often sublimated into actions that are also healthy and considered good. The lonely heart will either seek out people for friendship, sexuality, and other social activities; or it will withdraw and practice avoidance along with other defense mechanisms! The lonely heart will find activities like volunteering, serving on committees, mentoring, theater, and other community human services that put them around others and temporarily make them feel relief from their loneliness. Being a workaholic is still being a workaholic, even if it is unpaid and done on a volunteer basis! Some of the pillars in our local churches give their time like there was no tomorrow and gain great praise for their efforts, but they are doing it out of sublimated avoidance. Their hearts are lonely; they may even be avoiding their marriage partners or family with whom they are offended. They are unaware of their personal need for friendship, touch, as well as their total inability to function at a depth of relational intimacy, because their sublimation is covering their pain and weaknesses in this area.

Others simply do not know how to be at peace and be alone with themselves. They always have to be doing something, and they choose socially valued activities to avoid their internal tension. Either side of the sublimating coin leads to the repression of a heart that has some deep hurts and wounds that need to be healed and a heart that needs to be taught how to get their true needs met. The danger of sublimation is far less evident than that of some other defense mechanisms because the activities that are used to defend the heart emotionally are usually defined as socially "good." Nonetheless, the covering of the heart and its root issues that cause it pain go untreated and unhealed when this defense is used!

Take some time to list what your main drives and impulses are. Before assessing them as good or bad, allow yourself to see if you are wounded or have other core emotional needs unmet within you. Instead of covering your true desires and sublimating them unconsciously into socially acceptable means, you may be able to get a fresh revelation that the basic need and drive within you is to be loved! Your core need may be spiritual in nature and not just emotional. The need to feel safe, protected, valued, worthwhile, and unconditionally loved may be coming from "a God-shaped vacuum" that Blaise Pascal once said, is "in the heart of every man which cannot be filled by any created thing, but only by God, the Creator, made known through Jesus."

1. How do you sublimate, and what socially acceptable venues do you use to do so?

_____

_____

_____

_____

2. What emotional needs might you be sublimating, and how?

_____

_____

_____

_____

Sublimation

3. Have you acknowledged your need for touch? How do you get your needs for touch met?

_____

_____

_____

_____

4. Do you think that God can meet some of these needs that you have been sublimating onto other people and things? You can ask Him right now to speak into these needs and tell you whatever you need to know.

_____

_____

_____

_____

Chapter 19: Victimization

Victimization is a very difficult defense mechanism to share and confront because when someone is using this defense mechanism, they will often either respond with anger or withdrawal when it is exposed. Victimization is a defense mechanism in which the person uses a false perception of themselves being the designated object of consistent hurt and pain from others to justify and rationalize not taking responsibility for the healing of their own pain. This perception of being a victim of the evils of the world around them can lead you to remain fixed perpetually in your emotional pain, feeling sorry or pitying yourself for the state that you are in. Anyone who utilizes defense has likely been a true victim of some very difficult trauma in their past; their hurts are very much valid! However, victimization can be worse than the original trauma as it keeps you stuck in that pain for the rest of your life. Your trauma often becomes part of your identity when using this defense, as if what happened to you is part of who you were created to be.

Those who use victimization often tend to believe that they are martyrs. They think they were put on earth to be a sort of whipping post. Though we certainly have compassion for the person who uses this defense, they are taking on a mentality that will shape the rest of their life, a sort of self-fulfilling prophecy of negativity. The practice of victimization will make it harder for you to ever truly be healed from your trauma and pain. Rather than seeing yourself as a victim, you need to validate the pain that you have had and be empowered to get your needs met and move on to a better time in your life. Victimization as a defense is like if a person was in a car crash and stayed bleeding in their car, focusing on their bitterness toward the other driver who ran them off the road instead of going to the hospital and getting some medical attention. To deal with the cycle of victimization you must acknowledge the pain, but you also need to get help out of the car wrecks of life, get to the emotional hospital of support that will listen and counsel, and return to the driver's seat of life so your crashes do not become emotionally fatal!

Victimization can be subtle or very much overt. Here are some examples: The employee who was fired years ago may report that they have been fired multiple times unfairly and have given up on employment. Or the divorcee who was cheated on and becomes a kind of recluse because they were hurt so badly that they do not want to get hurt again, becoming depressed and fixated on how horrible their life is instead of going to a support group and getting vision for the next season of their life. Or the Christian who has seen hypocrisy in the church, and been the object of gossip or backbiting, and decides all churches are unsafe and that they will be better off to just watch church on TV once in a while because they could never trust people again.

Victimization as a defense is not so much about having negative emotions when someone gets hurt emotionally; that is natural and must be acknowledged and worked through. The key aspect of victimization is that you use that pain to rationalize your avoidance of doing anything about it. The victim will play possum; they will play dead as a defense against any further hurt. Victimization is really all about a person who doesn't take responsibility for themselves to work through their pain to prevent their negative circumstances from ruining their lives. It may sound like I am using defense mechanisms that I have previously debunked, but staying out of this defense is not just pulling yourself up by your boot straps or saying "stuff happens, oh well." The opposite of victimization is still acknowledging that there is pain and hardship, but also learning how to handle the evils of the world without getting stuck in an emotional pit of despair long term.

The Bible says that what a man believes in his heart he becomes (Proverbs 23:7), and this is personified in the one using victimization

Victimization

because they will project what they believe in their heart onto others and their surroundings until it comes true. They think they are a victim, and they then live life out as if they were a victim. Those with a victim mentality often exhibit a strong sense of self-pity; they believe that they will keep being attacked and rejected for the rest of their lives, so they feel justified in feeling sorry for themselves. There is fulfillment on some emotional level for those who feel they are a victim or a martyr! They feel some gratification in feeling cared for when others feel sorry for them too!

I can feel some of your defenses coming up as I write. Some of you have already denied that this could ever be you, others who have traces of this may be angry, and still others will now vow to yourself that you will *never* become one of these people. Please don't put up the walls. Most of us have used this, and all of these defenses, at different times in our lives. Taking a look at this defense may actually lead to your freedom and emotional health! If you do use this defense, it is no better or worse than any other, and it deserves a good looking into on your part to honestly evaluate your belief system. If you do find that you use victimization as a defense, you are taking great strides in just even admitting that to yourself. You can start to believe that you're "not a victim, but a victor!"

Isn't it bad enough that you have already suffered wrongdoing? It's time to take on your true identify as an overcomer (1 John 2:13) and walk through life outside of the fear that you will be hurt over and over again for the rest of your life! Though there may be some truth to your fear that the world is an evil place, you may also find that your hurt does not reflect who you really are, and your projections of being victimized in your future do not have to become your reality. Know that there are benefits you are trying to glean from using this defense and find out what they may be so you can choose to ditch this dangerous defense. Find helpful support that will validate you, listen to you, and empathize with you but at the same time ask you to take responsibility and at the proper time get you back into the saddle of life again to live and learn, walking out the pathway of life's wins and losses with hope for your future.

The Journey into the Divided Heart

1. Have you ever thought of yourself as a victim? What were some of the thoughts and actions that went with this attitude?

_____

_____

_____

_____

2. What might some of the benefits of being a victim be? What are some of the benefits to staying sick emotionally?

_____

_____

_____

_____

3.What would the opposite of this defense mechanism look like—to have the mentality of a victor?

_____

_____

_____

_____

Chapter 20: Dissociation

A significant stage in the journey of healing our hearts involves plugging into our hearts and identifying the pain that resides there from years past so we can invite healing into these places. In the midst of pain and trauma (which most have experienced on some level), we tend to learn to "dis" or "not" associate with ourselves, including our emotions and will. *Disassociating, or not associating, equals disconnecting from our emotional hearts.* It is a very common defense mechanism, hardwired in us by a merciful God and used automatically to protect us from overwhelming trauma. When we do not associate with our own hearts, it is no different than when we do not associate with others. We actively (though unconsciously most of the time) avoid and stay away from our own hearts with the purpose of managing our pain. I pray that God gives you revelation and understanding as you read. Revelation and application of these concepts to your life will open you up to new levels of healing and new levels of relationship between you and others!

Ed Smith of Transformational Prayer (formerly Theophostic Ministry)[5] defines dissociation as:

> *"A natural, God-created mind phenomenon in which conscious mental registry is either distracted or disengaged from what is occurring in the present moment. This behavior sometimes occurs during severe childhood traumatization."*

5. Smith, Ed M. *Theophostic Ministry (Advanced Training Series Level Two, Dissociation and Trauma Based Mind Control).* Campbellsville, KY: New Creation Publishing, 2002.

The Journey into the Divided Heart

Pastor Smith highlights that all defense mechanisms are "God-given," saying that "dissociation is not a problem to be 'fixed,' but is rather the person's solution ti their traumatic experience. Dissociation provides a mental escape from that which a person does not want to consciously experience, and eventually remember."[6] Dissociation is no different. Most psychologists say that dissociation is a base level, hardwired defense that is developed into splitting of identities mostly when trauma happens early on in one's childhood years." Dissociation is a God-given, natural way out of trauma used when the emotional pain is too much for the mind to handle in its present developmental stage. Dissociation is a natural process that happens automatically at the time of trauma, and in understanding this we can have much more compassion and empathy for those who are suffering through its negative consequences. Even though someone dissociates from their negative feelings in their conscious mind, their trauma-based thinking is still influencing their decision-making underneath the surface.

Pastor Smith also accurately labels dissociation as a "behavior" in the last sentence of this definition, which will help in understanding our interventions to avoid the pitfalls of such a defense. Categorizing dissociation as a "behavior" rather than an illness or a permanent condition allows us to realize that we are still choosing, even if it is on some unconscious level, to disconnect from our emotional self. If we can choose to use dissociation, than we can also choose to *not* use this behavior. Praise God! We will learn more about this in pages to come. Here is an example of how a friend with dissociation described the process of trying to stop choosing it as a defense:

> *You brought up in session about my willingness to not dissociate. It is hard not to do. It is almost second nature to me. Many times I do it without even knowing that I am doing it and lately, since exposing it, it's been worse. A lot worse! I feel like I am digging myself a grave. I feel like I am suffocating, but I'm not. I feel myself drawing back into myself and away from*

6. Quote from www.transformationprayer.org.

everyone and everything. I want to numb the pain emotionally and don't know how. Nothing is working.

And another describes:

I've ignored so many things for so long, that's honestly the only way I know how to survive…and it terrifies me to change it, not because I think it will be worse—I know it can be better. But I am afraid because in order to change it means I have to face my own demons; I have to face the fact that I am not as strong as I want to think I am. I've been comfortable in my pain because I have been able to somehow dissociate it away for a long time. I have never faced my traumas head on. I don't know how to do that without falling apart.

I thank these patients for sharing so vulnerably about the process of recognizing that we are choosing to use dissociation and that when we begin to recognize that we are doing so, we then begin to feel as though we are, as described above, "digging my own grave." It can feel "suffocating" to begin to choose to "face my traumas head on," and deciding to give up this and any defense mechanism can leave us feeling that "I don't know how to do this without falling apart." What feels like us falling apart, though, is actually us taking the first steps to come together as one integrated and whole person!

Many leading experts describe dissociation as a survival mechanism that is used to protect. It is activated by the nervous system when it reaches its maximum capacity to process internal and external stimulation and it serves to numb the body in order to feel less internal distress.

Take note that dissociation is labeled here not only as a defense mechanism, but as a survival mechanism to protect us from harm. The type and intensity of the harm that leads us to dissociate is experienced on a survival level, which means you could be going through physical life and death experiences, but even separations from our support systems when we are young can feel like survival issues. When the nervous system perceives intense emotional stimulation, it will automatically call up dissociative type defenses to take over in handling the emotions, thoughts, and memories of such events. The first times we use dissociation, then, are completely automatic and unconscious. Our hearts and minds use dissociation as the "defense of choice" when our emotional and physical existence is in question. Some might say, "But I have never been through anything truly life threatening that would lead me to feel that I may not survive." However, as you look at the world from a child's perspective (and at your own perceptions from when you were a child), you will see that any number of events can feel and look life-threatening. They include divorce of parents, relocation, losing loved ones including grandparents or pets, even being isolated from peers because of being picked on or rejected. Living life without the basic needs of security, safety, nurturing, a sense of belonging, and unconditional love can feel to a child equal to "I am not OK" to such an intensity that their continued existence is in question.

The definition above highlights one of the most common manifestations of dissociation by using the word *numbing* to describe the sensation in the body, emotions included. Persons who experience dissociation tend to describe it by saying that they feel "zoned out" or "checked out" or "foggy or spacy." They report feeling as though "I just don't care about anything." They share that they are "feeling like a robot some days" with no feelings at all. Other defense mechanisms begin to take over too, like intellectualizing, rationalizing, debating, and others, which can be quite frustrating to a flow of conversation of any depth with another.

There will often be times when the person with dissociation feels that they are experiencing "a tidal wave of emotions" whose source they cannot trace. Just as a dam holds all the water behind it unseen, these emotions will likely come spilling over at some point. Frustration, feeling overwhelmed, overstimulated, and bombarded are common terms that show that a dissociated heart is spilling the overflow of its emotions into the conscious mind of the divided heart. This can be really uncomfortable and scary to the people experiencing it. They feel as if their emotions and thoughts will not only overwhelm themselves but also the ones around them.

HOW DOES A PERSON GET TO THE POINT OF DISSOCIATION?

As previously stated, dissociation is a hardwired program in our biological computers given to us by God. It is a defense mechanism designed to protect us from the potential pain that is too much for us to handle in the dangerous world around us. God's Word teaches us that we will face tribulation of many kinds (John 16:33). These experiences can be more than we can emotionally handle at times. Dissociation is the mind's attempt to flee when flight is not possible. God gave us an emotional shock mechanism that gives us a way out of the pain when it is too much for us to handle. In a state of physical shock, our bodies shut down to such an extent that we can pass out and become unconscious to the world around us. God says He will not give you more than you can handle, and *"He will also provide a way out"* (1 Corinthians 10:13). Though we wish this meant that we would not ever encounter hardships that cause excruciating pain (emotional or physical), this is not the case. God gave us physical means such as shock to provide a way out. He has similarly given us an inherent emotional protective system in dissociation to give us a way out emotionally.

Here is an example of biological dissociation from an author who studies trauma responses in humans by comparing them to animals in trauma. In his book, *Waking the Tiger: Healing Trauma*[7] by Peter Levine, he describes the experience of his own dissociation when being attacked by a lion:

> *"It caused a sort of dreaminess in which there was no sense of pain or feeling of terror, though quite conscious of all that was happening. It was like what patients partially under the influence of chloroform describe, who see all the operation,*

7. Levine, Peter A. & Frederick, Ann *Waking the Tiger: Healing Trauma* Berkeley, CA: North Atlantic Books, 1997. 137.

149

but feel not the knife. This singular condition was not the result of any mental process. This peculiar state is probably produced in all animals killed by a carnivore, and if so, is a merciful provision by our benevolent Creator for lessening the pain of death. The best way to define dissociation is through the experience of it. In its mildest forms, it manifests as a kind of spacy-ness. At the other end of the spectrum, it can develop into so-called multiple personality syndrome. Because dissociation is a breakdown in the continuity of a person's felt sense, it almost always includes distortions of time and perception. In trauma, dissociation seems to be a favored means of enabling a person to endure experiences that are at the moment beyond endurance."

Dissociation then is a biological function with which we are all born! It is important to realize that humans and animals alike have been given these ways out of pain that is too much for us to handle at any given point in our development. *Thank You, God, that in Your benevolence, You put in us a mechanism to disconnect from physical pain. Thank You, God, that You gave us mechanisms to disconnect from emotional pain that is too great to handle as well.* God gave us this mechanism and hardwired it into our instincts to be accessed when needed, unconsciously and automatically.

Though I believe dissociation to be God-given and a hardwired response to turmoil built into our hearts from conception, when used outside of God's will on an ongoing basis it can also be the main barrier to living life to its fullest (John 10:10). Just as the physical mechanism of shock can in itself lead to death, so dissociation can in itself lead to emotional and spiritual death if untreated! As in shock, we need to raise the legs of the person suffering and get the blood flowing to the heart, so in dissociation we need to get nourishment and attention to the emotional heart. However, the process of coming out of shock and out of dissociation can be really painful as we begin to feel the pain of the trauma that happened to us previously, so there is usually resistance and new dissociation that happens in the healing process itself.

Dissociation

Dissociation is a means to handle the arousal and activation of our nervous systems by numbing and disconnecting us from experiencing this state of pain. When it is removed and healed though, it is common for the person to experience strong emotions that they are not used to having. This process of healing allows the pain to manifest more strongly and can often lead the person who is beginning to heal to turn back to the dissociated state that they have come out of because they are hurting so much. There is a time of being what psychology calls *hypersensitive* emotionally when coming out of dissociation, which makes the dissociated heart want to go back to its previous state of shock and dissociation. As a person comes out of dissociation, they are often hyper-aroused physically too and experience symptoms such as jumpiness, exaggerated startle response, cold sweating, rapid breathing, increased heart rate, loss of appetite, and difficulty concentrating. The healing process may even feel like what psychology describes as Post Traumatic Stress Disorder (PTSD), which is a state of having flashbacks and feeling the full intensity of past traumas in response to very small triggers. There can be trauma from healing from the trauma, if that makes sense. It takes great courage to pursue this path, but in the end, those who do will begin to feel like they are alive again for the first time since their trauma.

What does it feel like to have dissociation? Dissociation is most often experienced as numbness, coldness, and a general lack of emotion. If you have a lack of feeling and emotion, you may be dissociating! Others will notice these features in you much more easily than you, but if and when you dissociate, you will probably notice that it would be appropriate to have feelings when you do not. You may find yourself saying internally, "I feel really cold-hearted right now," or noticing that others are feeling emotions when you are not. A classic example of this defense at work is the person who just lost a loved one and is at the funeral talking about trivial matters as if they are in a coffee shop. This type of numbness is appropriate and normal in such a time of grief, but there is often an awareness in the one who is dissociating that their emotional lack is more than just he/she being in shock (the first of five stages of grief).

They will recognize that there has been a disconnect from their own emotions and feelings that is deeper than what others are experiencing.

The dissociated person will often realize that there is more to the picture than they are seeing internally, but they are mostly unable to access the information needed to explain the triggers that they experience in their everyday life. As described earlier, the dissociated heart is like a computer disconnected from the hard drive of stored historical data. To those who have dissociation, the triggers to them "should be no big deal," and they may have little to no idea why certain triggers are so intense for them. Dissociative people will feel an incongruence in their life, and an inconsistency too, that will leave them feeling kind of confused about why they do what they do.

Some have a fear of finding out that they have dissociation, so they use avoidance and denial to cover their symptoms. Dissociation is just another defense mechanism like the rest though, and it doesn't have to be feared! Dissociation is experienced on a wide spectrum of intensity and can be as subtle as you being forgetful or just daydreaming as a means of disconnecting emotionally. In fact, it can even be as subtle as driving down the street and realizing that you have passed three or four stoplights safely, like being on autopilot. I will share examples of dissociation in Dissociative Identity Disorder (DID, formerly Multiple Personality Disorder) and also will give examples of low level and subtle dissociation.

DID (Dissociative Identity Disorder)

When Sandy (concealed real name) came in to counseling at Renewal Center, she presented as a high functioning and very articulate young mother of three. Sandy assertively reported that she was having some marriage problems and was even able to take some responsibility for the anger that she was exhibiting toward her husband by saying that she needed to work on herself before bringing him in. Sandy began to tell of her life with John and the kids, and her triggers seemed to flow almost too easily as if her story was scripted and her responses premeditated. The answers were always very practical, given with a pretty flat emotional tone

152

and focused on her drive to find a solution quickly. After a few sessions of letting Sandy focus on problem-solving in the here and now, she decided to let me try some inner healing prayer ministry to get to the bottom of where this anger was really coming from.

Sandy and I went to prayer and asked Jesus to show us what was at the root of all of her anger. It wasn't more than a couple minutes into the prayer time that Sandy began remembering a trauma in her life that she had not been thinking of at all when she came in. She remembered being raped in the neighbor's basement as a child, and she allowed the emotions of this horrible memory to surface. (The *inner healing prayer minister does not lead people to specific memories, but sometimes God does.*)

As she began to experience the hurt, the horror, and all the pain of this memory, a sudden and distinct change in her demeanor and her mannerisms happened. Sandy was not being Sandy anymore! She looked up at me now suddenly with crossed arms and a defensive posture and said quite bluntly and with no emotion whatsoever, "Who the f— are you?" (I want to be honest about the wording to give you an accurate picture here.)

I calmly engaged this alter (or split of her personality) who was now speaking and replied, "I am Sandy's counselor and am here to help bring peace to painful places in her heart like the memory she was just talking about."

Sandy's alter just shook her head firmly, and with all certainty in her ability to direct our interaction, said, "Oh no, you don't! She (referring to Sandy) is not ready to go there! She is too weak and has been through enough already, hasn't she?" I explained that all I knew how to do was to take people to Jesus, and that Sandy had asked for inner healing prayer. I also added that Jesus was apparently bringing this up in her heart so that He could heal this memory and the pain that went with it. I knew that in our prayer, Jesus was given permission to take us where we needed to go, and this was where He had taken us! God will not turn down an opportunity to heal our hearts when we choose to "let go" because He loves us so much!

The Journey into the Divided Heart

This part of Sandy was what we call a "protector part" and was doing her job of protecting herself from perceived harm. I just happened to get a little too close to Sandy's wounded heart, leaving her feeling vulnerable to additional attack. This is what we see in people with distinct DID, but to some extent we also see this in the rest of us—a distinct change in which we instantly defend when our past hurts are triggered. To make a long story short, this protector part was willing to ask Jesus herself how to best protect Sandy's heart and was then willing to "sit on the sidelines" (which is what I call it when I am asking personalities to not go away, but just observe passively). This alter reserved the right to jump in at any time to stop the process if things were not safe and secure and I agreed compassionately and thanked the protector part for her work in trying to keep this abused heart safe. We always honor and respect people's splits and personalities for the work they have done in getting this person's heart through some very tough times! I continued to ask Jesus in an informal but verbal prayer what He would like to show us.

It was not much longer before the original alter who carried the pain was back and she was just as emotional as before. She seemed to pick up right where we left off, remembering some of the goriest details of her abuse. The pain can be very intense when we get to the place a trauma is stored! As she walked through the pictures in her mind of lying underneath this man who had complete power over her in that moment, I got to meet another part of her personality, who came forth in a distinct change of emotion, attitude, and posture. Instead of tears and fear, this new alter (the third one to present in our short conversation) began reporting her "disgust" with the "little girl that just laid there." This new alter spoke with anger and rage by saying, "I wish I could just kill her!" I didn't introduce myself this time as I was not addressed personally, but I did ask her why she wanted to murder her.

This alter was not a protector but a part in Sandy's mind that carried a self-hatred that she had not worked through. In this place she blamed herself—she "should have found a way out" of this circumstance (I have found this in some shape or form in most trauma survivors). She answered my previous question by saying, "Why do you think? She just laid there

154

like the weak little sh— that she is. She doesn't deserve to live, I tell you, she did not even so much as scream or kick! I hate her for that and will never forgive her!"

I know this gets confusing, but bear with me for a moment! Just as abruptly as this hate-filled part came, Sandy switched back to the broken little girl who was seeing herself being raped, full of hurt and fear; through her weeping and crying she said (to the alter who hated her), "I am so sorry! I could not even move! I could not even make a squeak! I was so scared that I think I just froze up! It is not my fault, I couldn't do anything." These are the symptoms of the trauma response of fight, flight, or freeze. In this case, the freeze mode had immobilized her.

The angry part and the frozen part went back and forth for a bit, debating what had never been discussed her whole life. She began to work through the dichotomy of emotions that had been too much for a little person's heart to handle during that horrific and unimaginable crisis in her life. In that one divided heart, Sandy was experiencing fear in one place, a sense of helplessness in another, and anger and revulsion in yet another. This anger and sense of retaliation never got acted out; it couldn't have because she would have been in even more danger. The anger was so strong and so dangerous to the situation itself that it had to be split off from the core of Sandy's heart, and it had stayed split from her until that day. This part had carried the anger at the other alters (herself) for not fighting her way out of harm's way. There was a host alter that had kept all of this turmoil and internal civil war buried underneath a facade. She had come to me as a strong and focused mom of three whose one goal was to press forward and find a solution to the anger that seemingly had to do with a simple set of triggers from her husband. Dissociation had helped her to survive but had also buried the real cause of her present symptoms from her consciousness. It had also kept her from being able to work through her trauma and it had affected her intimacy with her husband.

In prayer and through the safety that only God can bring to a time such as that, Sandy was able to begin sorting through the splitting of her personality and to understand the normalcy of having such a broad array of emotions internally that were in such conflict with each other. The protector part that tried to push me away could now begin to look at the means by which she protected as being an actual part of the problem. This part soon came to know how to *"guard your heart"* (Proverbs 4:23) in the way that the Scripture instructs us, without the anger and the isolation.

If you thought this was hard to follow on paper, you may well imagine what following someone who may have up to forty personalities operating back and forth from moment to moment is like. It can be extremely difficult! I will tell you, though, that there has been no work that has ever been more rewarding than seeing a heart divided at that level get healing and operate as an integrated and unified part of their community!

I hope this picture of dissociation reveals to you as the reader how different perspectives within the same heart can hold different realities and make differing free-will decisions for that person's life all at the same time. This is all happening in the unconscious. The host personality usually knows little to nothing of the true conflict happening internally (and does not want to know at some level). The result of the type of dissociation operating in a life like Sandy's is controlled chaos. Though healing is a very difficult process, the peace that comes internally on the other side of these defense mechanisms is the essence of all that our hearts are longing for. The example above with Sandy is an example of a person who struggles with dissociation on a clinical, diagnosable level called DID (Dissociative Identity Disorder). The healing that Sandy went through in a very short number of sessions was nothing less than a miracle!

HISTORY OF DID

There are accounts in literature of dissociative identities dating all the way back to 1791 when DID was described as having "exchanged personalities." In 1812, Benjamin Rush published his accounts of what we now call dissociation, having collected case studies of what he called

Dissociation

"doubling of consciousness." A review of the literature will find much in the early 1800s but the general public seems to have become aware of these symptoms of dissociation much later in history through a book and later a movie about a young woman who had thirteen "personalities" and was treated by her psychiatrist as she walked through the memories of horrific abuse she suffered under her psychotic mother and passive father. The intense and sporadic switching of alters that was represented in the movie by Hollywood left most people with a picture of DID that was highly dramatized and inaccurate. Most people with DID show symptoms at a much, much more subtle level that is often inconspicuous to those around them. The symptoms are subtle even to the person themselves!

Writings in the Christian church have just begun to deal with dissociation within the last twenty to thirty years, largely through those who have taught inner healing models as they further defined this obstacle that they found as they tried to help people. Some Christians have inaccurately treated dissociative identities as "demons" that need to be cast out. Well intentioned most of the time, the church at large has resisted a clinical understanding of the dynamics of the heart behind the symptoms, has misunderstood mental illness as a whole, and has often neglected or mistreated those suffering from this disorder. Can you imagine me trying to cast out Sandy's alter as if she were an "evil spirit" just because she had some anger in her? I have seen demonic spirits that do pose as a personality, but this is never to be assumed to be the case when "parts" of our hearts that need healing the most are hurting and often have intense symptoms like anger that need to speak.

Much of the church (like some of the psychiatric community) will tell you that this condition is largely fictitious, a sham, and rare to non-existent. No offense intended, but I have found that much of the church community wants to keep their head in the sand when they are asked to learn to recognize the symptoms of dissociation and to look for it in their churches. Unfortunately, much of the church community has made it unsafe emotionally for the DID to present in our local churches. The alters of the DID person will only present in our places of worship when

157

there is unconditional love and acceptance for who they are, and unless they present themselves there will be no healing for them. We in the church have (inadvertently) taught our people (DID or not) to conduct themselves as issue free whether they are or not! If you ever study this subject further, you will find that there are types of alters, and the types that some call "hosts" are more than happy to comply with keeping all their issues and symptoms hidden. Thus, when our "hosts" act as though they are healthy and whole, there is no exposure for the real pain inside, and the community and the church sees little to none of what is hidden beneath their "put together" exterior!

Denial of dissociation, exaggeration of its symptoms by the media, and the lack of general education of dissociation as a defense mechanism has led to dissociation being a painful and fearful subject that many use avoidance to stay away from. In general, people don't want to know they are dissociated because they are scared of the stigma. Our clinicians and doctors are often undereducated and skeptical of this disorder too. Even our church leadership is unconsciously and inadvertently working to facilitate dissociation by the way they portray Jesus as a man without emotion. The church will often teach people to demonstrate maturity, but they measure it by consistency of emotional stability, so most people learn to repress their emotions and pain so they are accepted by the group. We are going to work together and find ways to create a new future, though, where dissociation is de-stigmatized, normalized, and taught as being the defense mechanism it is, existing along a wide spectrum of intensities that we must learn about within ourselves.

If you have question about whether you or a loved one struggle with levels of dissociation, apart from the full diagnosis of Dissociative Identity Disorder, I have included the Dissociative Experiences Scale (DES) as an addendum in the back of this book so you can assess yourself more accurately.

DISSOCIATION AS A DEFENSE MECHANISM

Dissociation that is not diagnosable on the upper end of the spectrum of intensity can present itself on various levels from being very subtle to being just short of diagnosable, which we will categorize as simply the defense mechanism of dissociation. Just like the other defense mechanisms, this defense is not a diagnosis at this level. It does not mean you are mentally ill or crazy if you have this. Dissociation may be one of the most common defenses we use because it's a hardwired defense in us that is psychologically one of the most primitive, foundational, automatic defenses that we naturally have and use when the emotional heart is overwhelmed. The mind of a youngster going through pain and trauma does not have the capacity to rationalize, project, sublimate, or use most of the defenses described before this, so what do they do? They dissociate!

What does it look like to dissociate as a defense rather than a diagnosis? I always describe to people that dissociating is disconnecting from our hearts. We do it the same way we would unplug a power cord from the wall outlet. When we unplug from the outlet, the power is still there in the plug but we are not connected to it, and so is the dissociated mind unplugged from the emotions and memories and trauma that are stored in the heart and mind. Once unplugged, we not only do not have the feeling of the event, we often do not even have knowledge of the past event that the emotion came from. Again, this can happen on the most subtle of levels, presenting simply as forgetfulness, fogginess, or even that the person is a little flighty or airheaded. We compensate (a defense covered previously) well as adults and hide these symptoms by overachieving and distracting others who may notice. Those who dissociate will often very much connect with the fact that this defense is present when they learn how it works.

The subtle symptom of forgetfulness, as minimal as it is, may indicate the level of functioning that a person has. The person may not appear to be blanked out from their long or short-term memory, but they often will have difficulty functioning fully in some key areas. The more triggers, stressors, and relationships that are required in their life, the more easily some of that dissociated emotion may leak over into the consciousness and overwhelm their defense mechanism. Therefore, functioning at work can be very difficult. Most people who are dissociated have difficulty not only with work but relationships in general. Relational instability is a key to finding dissociation, though this can be due to many other dynamics too.

The dissociated heart is unable to access memories and trauma, but more obviously to those around them they are inconsistent and lacking in willingness or ability to be vulnerable in their relationships. Emotional blocks become relational blocks, and the divided dissociated heart is easily sniffed out by others who are more relationally functional. Additionally, memory is very important to life, and it is very difficult for those who use dissociation. Much of our memory is stored and organized according to our emotions, so one's memory is often not accessible when one's feelings are dissociated. This means that memory in random places and events begins to be inconsistent, emotions begin to be dissociated more and more randomly, and this leads people to try to cover their tracks. They then look defensive, hidden, and even as though they were lying as they try to make up for empty spots in their thinking. A person may look like they are not as intelligent as they are when they are dissociatedo, or they may look like the opposite as they compensate by overusing their intellect (intellectualizing).

Just asking people how they are feeling, to describe their emotions, and to choose to connect to their emotions is the start to learning how to overcome dissociation. The dissociated person is not just stuffing emotions, so don't assume that they know the emotion and are just burying it. The dissociated heart does not feel; it resists feeling, so when the dissociated heart is healing, it needs a lot of practice to teach itself alternatives to this defense mechanism. At our counseling centers we have kids and adults alike learn to "check in" to their emotions—to stop and choose to feel, pray through their blank spots, learning to pray and ask Jesus to help connect to them. We also lead them in mindfulness exercises to build their capacity to notice and cope with the feelings they do have when they decide to confront this defense inside of them.

Dissociation

I have had clients who cannot even identify their face in a picture of their family members as a child, whose full memory came back as they learned to give up dissociation. I have had many begin to reconnect to their dissociated emotions only to have very difficult memories of trauma follow shortly thereafter, affecting their sleep and shocking them with knowledge and memories that they have not had since childhood. Sometimes they don't believe their own memories, or they barely believe them. I have them give their memory the benefit of the doubt during this time though it may be distorted, which can be clarified later in the process.

I have had some who dissociate, reconnect to their hearts and begin to feel real love and depth of joy for the first time in their life too, as the dissociated heart usually disconnects from the positive feelings as well as the negative. It can happen fast, or it can be laboriously slow. Just have patience with yourself! I get into a lot of trouble with those I minister to because I give their hearts time but also a lot of responsibility regarding their dissociation, telling them that they are choosing to use this defense, even if unconsciously and habitually. They are choosing to not feel and remember, and they are challenged that they need to take steps to decide otherwise. I am then patient and caring, educational, and validating when they do not, helping them to see that they are frightened by what they may feel and remember. I also help them count the cost of staying dissociated, as they lose out on much more than they would ever gain from staying under this defense.

Complications that people experience when having dissociation can include sleep problems, poor self-esteem, feeling disconnected from yourself, mood changes that are unexpected or unexplainable, compulsive behaviors that you feel you just have to do, sexual problems, depression, anxiety, and suicidal thoughts. Some have the feeling that they have various self-talk voices in their head that seem different in tone and perspective. These may not be full alters, and they are most often not psychoses (delusions or hallucinations), but just different dissociated perspectives that your mind is trying to reconcile internally without success.

Dissociation is not a scary defense mechanism. Once you learn to recognize this in yourself, you will be able to move forward much more rapidly in your healing process. There is great hope for those who will work in this area, get help from friends, pastors, counselors, and choose to plug back in to their emotions. Long-term therapy clients, stuck in their progress, have been known to work through major past issues and get closure like they have never had before when they learn to get past the barrier of dissociation. Relationships can begin clicking and flowing naturally too, as two hearts plug back in to themselves and each other. I have seen people come off medications and discover amazing aspects of themselves that were buried away when they overcame their dissociation patterns. It is possible, and especially as you ask God for help you will find what the Bible calls, good *"fruit of your labor"* in this area (Psalms 128:2).

Last of all, I have a warning. When you let go of your dissociation, just like all of the other defense mechanisms, you will most likely experience new waves of emotions that may be quite unexpected. Dissociation, more than others, may create a kind of fear and shock in you as your heart has not been used to feeling the waves of emotion that may start flooding your consciousness. These waves may lead you to cry a lot! I have had some who heal to the point of coming into therapy and sharing that they do not really know why, but that they are crying and feeling waves of unexpected emotions in places and times that are not at all convenient for them. Though they are concerned and at times even afraid, as well as feeling as though they were taking giant steps backward, I am encouraged that they are peeling back the layers of dissociation and defenses that have covered the emotions that have been there all along. Patience, lots of journaling, and acceptance of this season of feeling like a melting pot of all kinds of dissociated feelings all at once will help get you through this time. Memories may begin to pop up that are true and not true, and you need to know that you do not have to understand them or prove them right or wrong. Just let the waves of emotions and memories come to the surface and remind yourself that this is a necessary step in the healing process. In the coming chapters we will talk about what to do next when you begin feeling and how to get to the healing. Before moving on, take a minute to ask yourself the following questions:

Dissociation

1. Did you take the DES test in the back of the book? What did you find? Do you show any symptoms of having DID?

_____

_____

_____

_____

2. Can you identify with any of the symptoms of dissociation as a defense? If so, which ones? How do you feel about having dissociation as a defense that you use? How do these symptoms negatively impact your life and your functioning?

_____

_____

_____

_____

3. Have you had any traumas especially before age eight that might have led to dissociation being developed in your heart? Name them and watch yourself to see if the feelings are connected or dissociated as you list them down.

_____

_____

_____

_____

4. Are you willing to choose to "check in" and give up dissociation as a defense? What is motivating you to give it up and why? Are you willing to ask Jesus to help reconnect you to your emotions and anything that you have unplugged in His timing? Are you willing to ask Him for help in sorting through all the emotions that you may experience on the other

side of dissociation? If so, pray right now, asking Him for help in your own words.

_____

_____

_____

_____

Chapter 21: Interventions

So what are you going to do about it? That is the question! What are you going to do with your divided heart? Maybe you have read these pages and decided that, "It's all good!" You think, "I've got no major issues and no defense mechanisms, really." If there is no conviction in these pages for you, then you are either leading a life head and shoulders above the rest of us, or maybe, just maybe, you have some defenses that your heart is not willing to recognize yet. I'm praying, though, that just like Jesus said of His disciples, your *"spirit is willing, but the body is weak"* (Matthew 26:41)! Maybe though, your spirit is willing despite your defenses and your hesitancy. You can do *all* things through Christ who gives you strength (Philippians 4:13), and these next pages are meant to give you some direction on how to pursue true and lasting change.

Each section could be a book in itself, but in summarizing and giving you some overview for direction I am certain that you, with the help of your close inner support circle, a good counselor (if needed), or pastor, and especially the Holy Spirit, will never be the same! If you will follow the interventions below, I can guarantee you that your life will change for the better. How can I do that? Not because I am any sort of a great counselor in myself, or because I am quoting someone who thought up these great theories on how to heal the human heart. I can guarantee there will be change because Jesus Himself promised that we would *"bear fruit"* (John 15:2) when allowing Him to prune everything that is not fruitful. These interventions are not just emotional and medical, they

165

are spiritual in nature—they put the Healer in charge of the healing! Healing is all about pruning the parts of your thinking and believing that are not fruitful, and there are steps we need to take in obedience to making Him our protector instead of occupying that role ourselves.

The following verse says this and more, and can be a truth to hold onto as you continue in your journey:

> *"His divine power has given us everything we need for life and godliness through our knowledge of him who called us by his own glory and goodness. Through these he has given us his very great and precious promises, so that through them you may participate in the divine nature and escape the corruption in the world caused by evil desires"* (2 Peter 1:3-4).

Isn't that encouraging? Jesus has already given us everything we need for life. We have great promises we can hold on to, and through these we can "participate" in the divine nature, which is not being depressed or anxious. God is for us and wants to give us life to its fullest (John 10:10)!

Before I describe some basic biblical tools for your healing process, I want to tell you a quick story that may help you *"count the cost"* (Luke 14:28 NKJV) of the road of healing ahead of you. "Counting the cost" is a term in the Bible that basically refers to considering how hard things will be before jumping in. Let's do that with this example.

The story that I want to share is the story of a fish affectionately named Skippy by my sister, Kris. Kris and I were at our elementary school fair where she won Skippy the Fish. As goldfish often are, he was handed to her in a small plastic bag of water; he was no more than an inch or two long. As good parents do, ours were more than willing to take in this newest little member of our family, but knew that the lifespan of a goldfish can be measured in weeks or maybe months. So they helped Kris pick out the smallest bowl possible (less than a foot wide and high) as well as a small bag of blue rocks that barely covered

Interventions

the bottom of the bowl that would become Skippy's home. Skippy made himself at home in his little bowl with blue rocks at the bottom and seemed content enough to swim in circles, having to choose only whether to swim clockwise or counter-clockwise for hour after hour of his pitiful little life.

Skippy had the cards stacked against him. He was a very small goldfish and his primary caregiver was a preoccupied little girl. To make things more difficult, he was introduced early on to our cat, Casey, who soon learned that he could drink from Skippy's bowl and liked to hunt—a lot! Sad to say, Casey's hunting practice eventually led to Skippy having only one fin to swim back and forth with. Skippy persevered nonetheless!

Though the average lifespan of goldfish is very short, and those that are hunted by an overgrown cat named Casey on a daily basis die quickly, Skippy lived on! In fact, Skippy made it through those first months and eventually grew to a size that now made it hard for him to even swim in circles. The bowl didn't shrink, Skippy had just grown and grown! Skippy continued to live on and grow bigger, and months turned into years, hanging out with Kris through elementary school, then middle school, through high school, and then even traveled back and forth to college with her strapped in the front seat, bouncing to and fro with each bump in the road. Amazingly, Skippy lived to be more than fourteen years old, still kept in his original bowl, with the same original blue rocks, living in the same small universe that he knew to be his world. Who would have known Skippy was filled with so much life?

Now Skippy had plenty of time to get to know his world around him in the small glass bowl and likely felt very comfortable swimming left or right year after year after year. I don't imagine that Skippy felt much anxiety (apart from his meetings with our cat) or depression, anger, or anything else uncomfortable. Though Skippy didn't likely feel his life was highly uncomfortable, I would like to ask you something. Do you think Skippy really lived life at all? Sure, Skippy was alive physically as evidenced by his not going belly up for fourteen years, but did he really live life, or did he simply exist? If living is interacting with the world around us, and his world was twelve by nine inches with no other fish around, no deeper waters to explore, no challenges to survive daily, no bigger fish that threatened to eat him, but also no love, no purpose, no victories, and no failures, I would say that Skippy merely *existed* and had no life whatsoever to experience! Life is about purpose, and what purpose was Skippy fulfilling in his limited and isolated little space? I feel bad for the little guy. His world was his prison, though he was comfortable and ignorant of all that he was missing compared to the rest of us; that bowl was actually a jail cell more than a refuge.

As you have likely gathered, I am comparing our lives to the life of Skippy the Fish and asking you to consider if you are willing to leave your comfort zones, your fish bowls, and enter into a world of potential harm that has emotional and spiritual challenges all around. We know that if Skippy was removed from his little fish bowl and placed in a bathtub that this new world would seem huge to him. He might even have freaked right out! In the bigger world of a bathtub, he wouldn't be able to see everything around him, and there would be deep waters beneath, and dark waters ahead and behind. The temperature would be different, the light different, and the predictability of his environment might bring worry to him as he interacted with the unknown for the first time.

What if we moved him to a small artificial pond in the backyard? The variables would be even larger and the risks much greater. We could add some other fish and let him experience racing other fish, playing tag, maybe even mating, fighting, and competing for food and space. How would Skippy feel then?

What if we took Skippy out into a real pond, with other bigger fish, birds, and all that would come with that environment? What if we put him in a stream, and then what if we put him in one of the Great Lakes? I know that Skippy's emotions would be stirred and he would be uncomfortable, but I also know that Skippy would truly live life in the world that God had originally put him in and would have potential to live life to its fullest (John 10:10).

Interventions

Some of you are thinking, "Give me the fishbowl! What a life, everything you want, and no risk, no harm, and all the security and ease that I want in my life." You may be thinking that would sound great because there would be no one to hurt you, no panic attacks, no rejection, just comfort and relaxation. No danger. No threats. Complete safety. You may even look at the sameness of that kind of life and think you would not mind being bored; you would be content with this simple life with its minimal risks. The interventions ahead will help you look at this, and where this need for false security at all costs is coming from.

The Skippy life in all actuality is a life that is incompatible with who Christ says you are. When you see yourself scripturally as more than a conqueror (Romans 8:37) and a force that is meant to take the world for God's kingdom (Matthew 11:12), you will be challenged from seeing the Skippy example through the eyes of your well-defended heart (Ephesians 1:18). Your defenses, as mentioned before, have become the problem, not the solution, the curse, and not the blessing. Jesus came to set the captives free, and your freedom must start with recognizing that your defenses are your captivity. This is not to say that you will be called to jump from the fish bowl into the big bad sea right away, but your ability to recognize your captivity and willingness to step outside of it is your first step! You have way more life in you than Skippy did, and you may be treating your life like we treated Skippy's—as though there wasn't much of a future ahead for him. What do you say, Skippy, you willing to make the jump? You willing to look to the future and all that God has for you?

It's scary to think that people would rather live in the little Skippy fish bowl that's safe and predictable than experience the world God created around them. This world needs you and your gifts and your skills; it needs you to make a difference for good! God said He created you to do *"good works"* before you were even born (Ephesians 2:10)! How can you do that while living in the fish bowl? Getting out of the fish bowl will bring you the true joy that we were created to experience and a realization of your purpose and importance in God's great plan! Those who are depressed and anxious may well be choosing captivity over the full God-given purpose that lies in the great expanse of the world God put us in. What they think is helping their depression and anxiety is actually causing it! When we shrink our own world or stay in the small world of our defense mechanisms, we are actually trying to be our own creators of peacefulness. In this, we are denying a Power higher than ourselves who has an amazing future and a full purpose for us on this planet.

Before reading the following life-changing concepts and praying the prayers given to get you started on new pathways, will you decide to leave your comfort zones, no matter how uncomfortable your emotions may feel? Will you take a risk and go for all that God has for you? John Wimber said that "faith is spelled R-I-S-K." Whether your life is in crisis and floundering in despair or whether you feel like life is going pretty darn well, I guarantee that there is a life outside of your walls and your defenses that will allow you to pursue heaven on earth (Matthew 6:10). However, it will take some faith to risk the emotional hurt that could lie ahead.

As Jesus said, *"The kingdom of heaven is near"* (Matthew 10:7)! That means that we do not have to wait to be dead to experience heaven; we are supposed to be living in heaven, in part, right here and right now while living on planet Earth. I hope you choose well. The costs of your decision are high for you and for those around you. Even though the costs are high, the Scripture says you are called to do *"even greater things"* than Jesus did (John 14:12). The question that leads us to our first intervention though is basic: Do you know the One who is the source of your healing? Do you have a relationship with your Savior, the one who wants to set you free? The Scripture says that salvation comes from no one else except through Jesus (Acts 4:12). Let's explore some deeper waters. Stay with me, all you Skippies out there, this intervention will get you to think about your beliefs and about your eternity!

Chapter 22: Salvation

T he story of creation leads us to the question of salvation and has everything to do with your emotional healing. You probably know the story, but we need to recap it to put this next section into context. Here is the short version. God created paradise—there was no evil, no sickness, no depression, no anxiety, and he put humans there to enjoy this paradise for eternity, starting with Adam and Eve. He called his creation, including Adam and Eve, *"good"* as we were made in His image (Genesis 1:31). Imagine that! We were made to be just like our God in His beautiful image! We were given one rule by God in the garden of Eden, and that rule was for our own protection. He was our protector from the beginning! However, Adam and Eve broke that rule and, in eating from the tree of the knowledge of good and evil (Genesis 3:6), acted on their desire to be *"like God"* (Genesis 3:5), with the consequence being that they were under a curse and banished from God's paradise in Eden.

We call this "the fall" because in Adam's act of disobedience to the perfect plan of His creator by the free-will choice that God purposefully gave him, we "fell" from the glory we were meant to walk in to a much lower state of being in sin. The Bible says that we have all sinned; this is defined in Scripture as falling short of the glory, or the fulness, of God (Romans 3:23). We were meant to walk in the fullness and the wholeness of who God is, having intimacy with Him. This relationship would have fulfilled all our needs.

What were we to do after the fall? After breaking God's one rule, Adam and Eve had no access to their garden; they were now in a fallen state. They came under the curses listed in Genesis 3:16-19 and lived with "the knowledge of good and evil," which led them (and now us) not to a reliance on a loving God, but to a reliance on self. This self-reliance brought with it the attitude that we don't need anyone, including God, to rule our lives. As previously shared, we see defense mechanisms abounding immediately after this fall in the garden. Adam and Eve covered themselves with fig leaves, hid from God, rationalized their decision-making, and denied their responsibility in the process of following the serpent instead of the good God they knew. The fall brought all of this. It brought pain in labor for Eve (Genesis 3:16) and the breakdown of relationship in the family to the point that Cain murdered his brother Abel (Genesis 4). As we read their story, we see pride, sickness, confusion, and ultimately such evil abounding in the earth that God eventually regrets that he even created mankind. The fall messed up everything, and God wiped out the whole earth in a flood, saving only Noah and his family on the ark.

According to the Bible, the origins of what we suffer—including sickness, mental illness, anger, anxiety, depression, relational problems, and pain—are all a result of this fall! But it did not end there. God is wise and wonderful. He had made a plan before He even created us to save us if this happened. In fact, He knew it would happen, but it was important to Him that we have a free will so we could choose Him. His plan was perfect. The plan was not to somehow lower His standard, which would go against who He inherently is, but the plan was to grant a solution to the problem that Adam and Eve created by their disobedience while keeping His standard of holiness.

That solution in the Old Testament was that our sins and our fallen state would be paid for by sacrifices to God. The most powerful sacrifices were those of animals sacrificed to God by the priest on the temple altar. Scripture says that there is life in the blood (Leviticus 17:11) and sin leads to death (James 1:15), so our choices leading to death needed to be paid for in blood to bring us life. This plan of sacrificing animals was set up only temporarily by God and in the long run was specifically meant to reveal His heart toward us in that He was willing to send His

Salvation

own son, Jesus Christ, as the sacrificial Lamb for our sins (1 Peter 1:19). His plan to "redeem" us was to offer what was closest to Himself—His only Son—to "buy" back the freedom and the life and the paradise that God created us to live in before the fall. Jesus would buy all that back for us with the great cost of His own life on the cross. Just as Aslan gave his life willingly on the altar for Edmund in C.S. Lewis's *The Lion, the Witch, and the Wardrobe,* Jesus gave Himself over to evil to be killed in order to pay for our sinfulness. Our Savior Jesus gave Himself to buy us back from the powers of darkness, hanging on a cross and shedding His blood to set us free. That's right! We can be *free!*

Much, much more could be said here, and my hope is that you will study the original plan of the God who created you and me to be free and live in paradise with Him. My great hope is that you would study the Old Testament, its laws, and how it was all set up to point to the true solution to our sin—Jesus. The Bible reveals who He is and what He truly did for you on the cross that day. My prayer is that you would have revelation that your sin is not in your behaviors alone, but that it has its origin in your great, great, great, great, great...grandfather Adam who first allowed sin into our world through his decision. Our fallen condition was a hopeless state that we put ourselves in as humans by living outside of God's perfect plan for us, starting way back in the garden of Eden. My goal is that your first intervention in this healing process would be to give yourself back to that original plan set up for you by God. You can have fellowship with God like it was in the garden again, but this can only be done as you accept His Son, Jesus, as your Savior.

Accept Jesus as my Savior? Savior from what? *Saved* means rescued, but rescued from what? Rescued from all that came into our world and into our nature when Adam departed from the original, glorious, and holy plan that our Creator intended for us in the beginning. God's original plan was for you to live life to its fullest without sin, sickness, mental health symptoms, or broken relationships. The only way back to this place is through accepting the free gift of God, Jesus, as the sacrifice for your sin. You can do that today for the first time if you have not ever prayed for a relationship with Him before. You can also pray this prayer if it is your thousandth time because our healing process will only be truly successful in the sense of us becoming whole by starting at this place.

This Jesus, the One who gave His life for us as a free gift from God, needs to be received not only as our Savior, but also as our Lord. *Lord* means master. Yes, our defenses do not like that word. That word in itself signifies giving up control and trusting Him enough to submit ourselves as a slave does to His master. We have a good master though, but our defenses are not used to thinking in terms of the freedom we gain when we fully trust and submit to Jesus. We are not only submitting to His ways, doing things His way as He directs us, but we are submitting to His heart, which from the beginning has always had the best for us. He is a good, good Father who wants the best for His kids, and if you have not experienced having a good earthly father, then your traumas and defenses will likely fight this decision of following Father God through accepting Jesus as your Lord. But our heavenly Father is not like our earthly ones. Aren't our divided hearts example enough that we need something and Someone greater than us to be healed? In receiving Him as the answer to our fallen, broken, divided state, we are acknowledging that God's way is the better way. We accept Him then as our Savior and as our Lord, and ask Him to lead us *"in the way everlasting"* (Psalms 139:24).

Scripture says that we are redeemed by Him! Think of redeemed in terms of a coupon that we redeem by turning it in at a store to claim the benefit that is promised on it. We verbally and in prayer to Him turn in our coupon (Jesus), which states that because of what Jesus has done for us, we are promised all the original rights and privileges that come with being restored to the original state in which we were created by God. So it is time to decide to pray, because the coupon does you no good if it is not cashed in! I will have you pray a simple prayer of redemption, as I will give for each of our interventions, and give you the chance to decide to start your healing process right now by beginning this journey with the Healer as your trusted guide.

Salvation

Let's pray by saying out loud:

"Jesus, I come to You now as Your creation and as Your child. I ask You to come into my heart now as my Savior and redeem me from my fallen state. I ask You to forgive my sins, and the sins of my generations before me, and be my Lord whom I will follow for the rest of my days. I ask You to apply Your blood that You shed on the cross to all my shortcomings, and I lay claim to Your promise that I will be saved from sin, from sickness, from symptoms of mental illness, and from all that was not a part of Your original plan for me. I give You the authority in my life to lead me and guide me, and I ask that You would help me to build a fresh and new relationship with You—one in which I would know Your great love in every place inside of me where there is pain and no peace. Thank You for the sacrifice You made for me on the cross. Please come live in my heart from now forward. Amen!

The Bible says that if you believe in your heart and confess with your mouth that Jesus Christ is Lord, you shall be saved (Romans 10:9), and so if you did that today you are starting afresh and you have a new and changed life that starts today and continues on into eternity with Him forevermore! Awesome! Now get in a church, study, learn, and talk to your Savior and your Lord every day. The adventure in front of you will require support and training so you can grow well in this place that you have decided to live in today!

Notice the new softness that you have even now and the different perspectives you have on life since you prayed. You are different! Test it out. Think of the people with whom you have been angry and see if your heart is not softened toward them. Look inside where there was hopelessness and despair and see if there is not hope and even joy there now since you prayed!

Though you will have temptations to go back to doing life your way, there is now a new nature in you to do things His way! Not a "fallen nature" but God's original plan-A nature that wants to be like Him, the

The Journey into the Divided Heart

One who created you. Learn to receive His love to fill the empty places inside of you and to release all your cares and worries to Him. It would be good to stop and journal some of what you have felt in making this decision and praying this prayer. Do you feel hope, peace, love? If so, that is the inner working of your Savior showing you that He is the answer to all that you have been struggling with. Where there is still no peace, the following interventions are needed to take the next crucial steps in your all-important journey.

Chapter 23: Repentance

T hough these interventions are not your typical ten steps to freedom, they are spiritually life-changing understandings that are central to living life to its fullest (John 10:10). This next intervention, repentance, will get you on the right path and keep you there. It is one of the big guns in your arsenal, so learn to use it well.

As we come out of reliance upon our defenses, we can come into a place where joy, peace, and love replace depression, anxiety, and other negative mental health symptoms. Changing our thinking is the cornerstone of the skills needed to be able to move forward in this emotional healing process, and that change in our thinking begins with repentance. It is important to know how change happens, and, as has been mentioned earlier, Scripture is clear that we are transformed by the renewing of our minds (Romans 12:2). In fact, before starting the counseling center I now own and run, I asked God to tell me as if I had never learned a thing in my life and career, "How does a person change emotionally?" His quick answer was Romans 12:2, which highlights the importance of changing or "renewing" our minds. This is why I called our counseling agency "Renewal Christian Counseling Center," and this is why I believe repentance is foundational for how you will see true change in your life. We can learn to cope, and we can gain some skills and counseling tools in clinical counseling alone, but we can only be transformed by the renewing of our minds through intervention by the Counselor Jesus Himself! Do you want to learn to cope, which means by definition to put up with or to live with your symptoms, or do you want to be transformed and changed permanently?

What Romans 12:2 is saying is that change essentially happens by addressing our mind and the way that we think! In the passage in Romans, the last part of the verse is telling us the outcome of this transforming process more specifically. The end of the process is that we would know the good and perfect will of our Father. In other words, we take our old attitudes, beliefs, and thought patterns, and we replace them with His thoughts!

Psychology relies heavily on what we call cognitive behavioral therapy (CBT), which essentially says that we change our emotions and behaviors by changing the thoughts and beliefs we have internally. The behavioral part of CBT basically means that we have to act out our new beliefs rather than just talk about them, which we will talk about in the next pages. CBT agrees exactly with Romans 12. God is teaching cognitive behavioral therapy in Romans 12:2, and is putting Himself right in the middle of that process, as He should be. The great addition to traditional CBT that we have as believers is that we know we have a God who always trades up and gives us something better than we give Him: *"beauty for ashes"* (Isaiah 61:3 NLT). He takes our "stinking thinking" and trades us our old thoughts for new thoughts that are able to bring true love, true joy, and true peace. CBT without renewed truth-based thinking can be of no use. If our minds trade in a wrong thought for another wrong thought, we will not get better; we will not change. Only God-centered CBT is of any value because God promises: *"You will know the truth, and the truth will set you free"* (John 8:32).

Repentance is the most crucial part of the cognitive behavioral therapy that we all need. Repentance simply means "to change your mind." Changing our behaviors and emotions does not happen by just talking about them but by changing the thoughts behind the behaviors; these are the root of our symptoms. Repentance starts with acknowledging that our thoughts need to be changed. The humility of this process makes us teachable, trustworthy to others, and free inside to grow and learn without feeling shame.

Many who have had a strong religious background will equate the word *repentance* with a feeling of guilt and shame that they learned. They were taught that we repent because we are "bad" and need to be "punished." If this is your experience, then you will likely be having many defense mechanisms come up as you read. Like my pastor always says when talking about our negative thoughts, "You are not bad for having these thoughts. You are just wrong." How does it feel right now to think that you're not bad? How does it feel to think that oftentimes you are wrong (especially in your thinking)? If there are negative emotions there with the thought that sometimes you are wrong, then this is a place in your divided heart that needs some ministry and healing. This is a place that needs revelation that it is not only OK to be wrong, it's been the norm for mankind ever since the fall.

We can have wrong thinking and be in need of repentance, but this doesn't mean that we are bad or that we need to live in shame. God's intent is not to punish you or to tell you that you're a horrible person. God's intent is to bless you and teach you how to think His way. His way of thinking is higher and more effective than our way of thinking. It leads to the peace and joy that are the opposite of what we experience in our depression and anxiety.

We need to look at the progression of this renewing of the mind and see that it happens on four different levels. True thought transformation happens only as we get to the bottom layers of the following illustration.

The Journey into the Divided Heart

Look at these four levels as a building. We can only change the security of a building by working on the foundation all the way at the bottom. Everything depends on that foundation. As the illustration goes, our behaviors are what is seen from the surface, and they are at the top. Our behaviors do not originate from themselves though; they come from the layers below. They come from our emotions, and likewise our emotions come from our thoughts. Without a thought, you do not have an emotion. That is an important point for you to remember. If you really want to change your emotions from being depressed, angry, and anxious, you need to be willing to work on your thoughts. A changed thought leads to a changed emotion because an emotion is nothing more than a reflection of the thoughts that are going through our heads.

Our thoughts come from our beliefs. Some people in counseling and inner healing are willing to talk about their emotions and vent, but not many are willing to truly look at, and change, their internal belief system. I hope that you are one of the few who are willing to go there. I always tell my counselors this sad truth: We see about one in ten clients who really are willing to follow the change process through to the foundation level of changing their beliefs. I am praying that you are one of those in the ten percent.

Let's go through the process of repentance and make it more practical. I will add this intervention to the end of the CBT process in the following example. Hypothetically, let's say a guy named John gets home from a long day at work and sees that there is no dinner on the table. As he begins to interact with his wife who has been home all day, John acts irritated and short with her. When she asks him if he is OK, he says something angry and belittling like, "Probably not as good as you are." (This is his behavior and a sarcastic defense as well!) Mapping his behavior to where it has come from makes us ask, "What is John feeling that is leading him to act this way?" His feelings are more than just him being irritable. If we really look in John's heart, he may be able to tell us that he feels frustrated that he had to work all day and that his wife did not even have dinner for him. He might even be able to gain insight and name his emotions: He does not feel any respect for his hard work and he feels unimportant to his wife.

If we really want to help John, we need to keep following our chart and go to the next floor of the building by asking him, "Why do you feel this way?" John's feelings, like all of us, come from his thoughts. John, like many of us, may not be able to tell you his feelings or his thoughts right away, though, because of his lack of insight and the defense mechanisms that cover his heart.

If we are able to map John's thoughts out further, we will see that John is feeling disrespected because he thinks he has been "wronged" and he is also offended, comparing himself and his busy day to what he perceives as his wife's lazy day. He has come to a conclusion and a judgment in his mind. This results in his anger because he doesn't feel he is being treated right. He may have thoughts like, "This is not fair," and "If she loved me, she would have dinner waiting for me on the table when I got home from work."

Following the building example to the foundation, we need to ask, "Where do these thoughts come from?" John has a belief system somewhere beneath these behaviors, feelings, and thoughts that defines the roles and the expectations of a wife who "loves" her husband. These beliefs will be firmly embedded in the programming of John's mind like software loaded into the hard drive of a computer. This is because he probably learned them long ago and validated his beliefs by what he observed as he grew up. Maybe his mother always had dinner ready for his dad, so should his wife then treat him. It will not be easy, but to bring peace to this situation and all the other triggers in this area between John and his wife, we will have to challenge John's beliefs and ask him to consider that his beliefs may be wrong, or at least incomplete. Would you be willing to be challenged like this if you were John? Or would you be offended and defend your divided heart? Take a moment and look at the times when you have been upset lately. Remember the more personal trigger points you have had that are much more upsetting than this simple example?

181

The Journey into the Divided Heart

It's time for John to get out of the fishbowl though! At this point in the repentance process, it is time for him to "change his mind"; this equals repentance. It is time for John to make a free-will decision based on his motivation to grow personally, spiritually, relationally, and renew his mind. Repenting, at this point, begins with John being willing to put a question mark behind his belief that "if a wife loves a husband she will always have dinner on the table for him after work." If he is able to see that this is not necessarily true by himself, or through conversations with pastors or counselors, or even directly through the conviction of the Holy Spirit speaking to him, he can now move into a place where he gives up his old belief to God and asks for a new way of thinking. If he does do this, there is great potential to see that even though he did not have dinner waiting for him, he is loved and even respected by his wife!

My favorite way to direct the repentance process is simply to ask a person like John to take his beliefs and thoughts to prayer. When John takes his belief to prayer, he is asking God Himself if it is true that his wife's love equals her having dinner on the table for him after work. This interaction between us and God is outlined in Scripture as being what Paul (an author in the New Testament) calls taking every thought captive, and we are told to then change our thought to agree with Christ's thought (2 Corinthians 10:5). My initial goal in helping John take these thoughts captive would be to have him ask Jesus in prayer, "Jesus, is my thought true?" Our scriptural mandate is actually to do this with each of the thoughts and beliefs behind our negative behaviors and feelings. This may seem trivial to you, especially in this example, but this is God's way to handle our thoughts according to His word. How much more fruitful this process is when a sexual abuse survivor or other wounded heart hears from God. It is powerful when He says something like, "No, it was not your fault," or "I see you blameless and pure." That divided heart will be a lot less divided after hearing that truth!

Asking, "Is that true, Jesus?" will only work if we are willing to hear Him and let ourselves hear the good and perfect will of the Father (Romans 12:2). He will tell us in prayer what we need to hear if we will just listen. Many of us do not have this type of relationship with Jesus though. Many would struggle to hear His voice speak truth into this situation. Others hear Him well and that is great! If this is the case, we can simply ask ourselves when taking these thoughts captive, "What do I think Jesus would say?" Some of us will be able to ask and hear clearly the voice of our Father God because we believe and have practiced walking in what the Scripture says—that we are like sheep, and the sheep know the Shepherd's voice (John 10:3). It is not psychotic to hear the *"still small voice"* (1 Kings 19:11-13) of our loving Shepherd. Just know that voice is not His when it is cruel and condemning. Then it should be challenged with the help of our counselors, friends, and pastor.

The Scriptures will help greatly in this process of repentance of thoughts too, and in John's case we could look at God's definition of love in 1 Corinthians 13 in which the Bible does not say that love equals "getting dinner on time" (yes, there is a bit of sarcasm in my words); it says that love is more a matter of the heart when a person is patient, kind, and keeps no record of wrongs (1 Corinthians 13:4-5).

I hear plenty of situations like this all day long. When people ask God questions like this, He often replies in a still small voice, "She loves you very much and it is you who is judging her." God will convict us of our need to change our attitudes and thoughts and challenge us as the Scripture says to *"take the plank out of your own eye"* before we see the speck in our brother's (Matthew 7:3-5). If you do not hear God's voice this clearly, it is time for you to develop your relationship with Him to a point where you can discern what He is saying to you on a moment-by-moment basis. Yes, this is possible and is a key to your healing. Don't let hopelessness tell you otherwise!

Repentance will become a part of your everyday life. You will begin to notice, like in John's case, every time you are not at peace and we will be able to work through these steps to get to the faulty foundational beliefs that you possess so you can exchange them for God's truth moment by moment. This process of repenting and renewing your mind can and should happen without shame or guilt, bringing life and joy and love and peace! Psychology calls this cognitive process I just described "reality testing" the thought (which is exactly what we are doing) and

The Journey into the Divided Heart

calls it "cognitive restructuring" when we change that thought to another more accurate belief, which is also exactly what we did when repenting. I guess Jesus believes in cognitive behavioral therapy too.

It is decision time now. Are you willing and ready, no matter how wrong you think others are, to own your own emotions and thoughts? Are you ready to take ownership and responsibility for your thoughts and repent for them, replacing them with God's truth instead of blaming others and saying, "They made me feel (fill-in-the-blank)"? I promise you, if you make this repentance process a part of your everyday thought life for every belief and thought that is not peaceful and loving, your divided heart will be on the fast track to healing! If you are willing to begin this process of giving up your old ways of thinking and taking on God's new ways of thinking, then let's pray and get out of the Skippy bowl of staying stuck in our present set of beliefs. To get started, pray the following:

Father God, I come to You today full of pride that is evidenced in the way I believe my way of thinking is above Your way of thinking. I come to You acknowledging that I have believed so much in my own way of thinking that I do not often stop to even check if my thoughts line up with Yours. I choose today to begin taking every thought captive to obey You, to discipline my thoughts so I can repent for those that are leading to negative feelings and behaviors in my life. I take responsibility for my "stinking thinking" and ask You to begin renewing my mind and my thinking by convicting me when my thinking is not in alignment with Yours. I choose to change my mind when I see that my thoughts are not right, and I ask You to replace every belief that leads to depression, anxiety, anger, and relational difficulty with Your truth that "sets us free." I commit to living a life of repentance today, and I ask for Your help to stay humble and teachable instead of being defensive and walled off. I thank You for Your help, oh God, and for the blessings that will result from living this life of repentance starting today. Amen.

Chapter 24: The Power of the Will

D id you know that you have one of the most powerful forces in the entire universe inside of you? You have a free will! That free will is, in some ways, even more powerful than God! Pretty crazy, huh? You may be thinking, "How so?" God has given us a free will, meaning that we are inherently given freedom by our Creator to make our own choices, good and bad. This means that God has not made us like robots that will just do what He wants. God has promised that He will not override our free will decisions even when our free will leads us toward paths He does not want for us. He will not override us even when our decisions are harmful to ourselves and to others. For some of us, that is kind of scary, and we wish God would just take over our will so we could just do things His way, but that is not how He set things up. Our will is just another name for our desires, pleasures, and wants, and it is from this will inside of us that we make our decisions regarding what we do and don't do. We are truly free to choose!

Our will is to us what a transmission is to a car. It's the part in us that like a transmission in a car controls the power of the engine and determines what direction that engine will take us. This transmission is a powerful and empowering part of who we are, and harnessing it will lead us to great freedom. It does need to be broken and humbled though. Like a wild horse that has a strong will of its own, we need to turn our free will away from doing whatever it wants to do.

185

The Journey into the Divided Heart

The good news about this is that just as easily and subtly as we choose a defense mechanism, we also can also choose to not use a defense mechanism. Just as easily as we choose to dissociate, we can choose to not dissociate. Just as easily as we chose to live in denial, we can choose to come out of denial. Choice is a choice! We can choose to make choices and accept that we will live with the consequences and rewards! We can choose to come in and out of operating in all of the defenses listed in the previous pages; thus, we have the choice to live a life exposing our hearts to the world outside our castle walls or to live inside the castle walls using all our self-protection to keep the world and God at bay.

I am not saying that we are always aware of the choices we are making, as we are in denial of our denial at times too. I get lots of people mad at me by reflecting to them the free will choices they are making because they have not trained themselves to be aware of the subtle choices they are making internally every moment of their day. Often they feel bad about themselves (cognitive distortion) when they see how often they are using defense mechanisms and making internal judgments about others. They often defend their heart with denial or anger instead of just learning how to use their transmission to make better free will decisions inside!

I am also not trying to preach to you that our emotions and thoughts will line up with this concept of choice and that once we make a choice that it will always feel all nice and cozy inside. Our emotions and our thoughts have much to say about how hopeless it is to even try to change, how scary it will be living in vulnerability, and how much rejection and hurt we are inviting into our lives. We do have a free will and can choose to put the transmission in forward, but will often have to tell our minds, our body, and our emotions to shut up! In true healing, we will often have to move in a specific direction even though it feels really crappy to do so. As Joyce Meyers says, we often have to "do it afraid!" This means that we choose to do things despite our feelings of fear, in order to find that we are really OK in the end.

The Power of the Will

I do not have to listen to my thoughts and I do not have to listen to my emotions. It is important to learn to discipline our behaviors, but even more important to learn to discipline our emotions by our free will and to not let them be the full guiding force of our lives. Emotions are not bad in themselves, but I am empowering you today to stand against your feelings and choose to not put them in charge of your life. Use your free will, your transmission, to move in a new direction and see where that path may take you. That means that even when your emotions tell you that you have been hurt and they want you to run away and withdraw from everyone, you can choose to not run from your relationships but run to those relationships instead, preventing the division that would otherwise result!

We talked about trauma earlier. Many of us have Type A trauma (neglect) as we were not disciplined lovingly by a parent who taught us not to let our emotions be in the driver's seat. If that is the case, be patient with yourself, as this will take a little more time. But rest assured, you can change and you will feel much more stable when your free will learns to say no to your feelings. It is time to *choose*, and time to take authority over your life by "choosing to choose" not just what your feelings tell you to do. You can start by putting Jesus in control of this process as you did in the salvation section. You can be as Joshua in the Old Testament who said to the Israelites:

> *"But if serving the Lord seems undesirable to you, then **choose** for yourselves this day whom you will serve, whether the gods your forefathers served beyond the River, or the gods of the Amorites, in whose land you are living. But as for me and my household, we will serve the Lord"* (Joshua 24:15).

Let's exercise our free will now, discipline our emotions, and put our transmission in forward, praying the following and then choosing to walk this prayer out until our character reflects a consistency and a stability to overcome anything that depression and anxiety throws at us.

The Journey into the Divided Heart

Dear Lord Jesus, I come to You with my free will acknowledging that I need You and Your help with my divided heart. I know that You have given me a free will. Out of this free will, I decide this day to serve You as my Lord. I choose to listen to Your voice over my emotions and to ask You to bring understanding and direction to my mind. I choose to feel the emotions in my heart without reliance on my defense mechanisms, and I ask You to keep my free will humble and soft in this process of healing that I am pursuing. I now decide in my free will to take down my defense mechanisms. I repent of my avoidance, addictions, anger, projection, dissociation, and all other walls that I may have used in the past. I choose to give these up as my protection, and I ask for Your help in recognizing when they try to come back up. I know that I have been empowered by You since the beginning of creation with a free will that has the ability to choose rightly, no matter what I feel or think. Thank You, Lord Jesus.

Chapter 25: Reframing

Did you ever buy a picture to hang on the wall and just not have the right frame for it? I shopped far and wide for the perfect painting to go in my office, to set the mood and to encourage my clients. I wanted something to bless them and give them hope for all that God has for them. I found some prophetic art (which is a picture inspired by what one of God's children saw in the Spirit) and it seemed perfect. I took it to the store and bought one of those cheaper frames (yes, I am too frugal at times; it is a defense mechanism that helps curb my fear of lack of provision. I'm working on it!), and guess how much I liked it? It actually took away from the overall scenery of the picture, and in some ways even skewed its meaning. I took it back and spent a little more money (in faith, I took a risk). This frame had a fancy, beautifully carved, wooden scroll pattern in it. Guess how much better the picture looked? Now the frame matched the picture and spoke a consistent message of grandeur and inspiration. I love it, and my clients do too!

This next skill that is crucially important to the healing of your divided heart is called "reframing." It means that you can do to your thoughts and perceptions what I did with the picture in my office. You not only can, but you must if you want to protect your heart God's way without the defense mechanisms that hinder you. It is not only the goal of therapy, recovery, or inner healing to just let our guard down and be vulnerable to the world around us. The goal is to see and perceive the world around us more accurately so we do not just react based on perceptions. Our perceptions may or may not be completely accurate.

The Journey into the Divided Heart

Just as an umpire in major league baseball can now get a replay and see things from all kinds of different angles to make an accurate call on the field, so we need to see the circumstances of our lives from many different angles so we can make the right call on the plays of our lives.

It is common in therapy to see a client who is obviously (to me, not to them) skewed in their perspective, and it is sad to see the decisions that come forth from these faulty perspectives. For instance, it is not uncommon to see a married couple in counseling where one spouse believes the other to be unfaithful. Now, just for the record, I know that our culture has a definite problem with faithfulness. I am not too naïve to explore the possibilities when these complaints are rendered. It would be really ignorant to assume that anyone is above lying and cheating. However, there are those who are so obviously skewed in their thinking by their past traumas, hurts, and affairs that they see everything through dark-colored glasses, which paint pictures for them that just are not true. Simple and highly explainable circumstances can be framed by the insecure spouse as an obvious sign that the other is cheating. I have unfortunately seen many of these situations in which a spouse ends the marriage and beautiful families are broken up based on no evidence whatsoever.

It is not only in marriage that our perceptions get skewed, but in life in general. Excuse my French, but as my seventh grade math teacher always said, "When you assume, you make an 'ass' out of 'u' and 'me.'" These skewed perceptions that we have can make a mess out of any situation and within any relationship. Parenting in particular is prone to seeing kids and situations through faulty and skewed perceptions, so are workplace issues, church situations, authority issues, friendships, and even our perceptions of ourselves. We need to make sure our pictures are put in the right frames!

Reframing is the skill that takes what you think to be fact and challenges whether it is truth. What is fact is not automatically truth. That husband might have had an article of women's clothing in his car, which is fact, but the truth may be that it is his sister's and she left it in the car when he took her to work the night before. Your friend may have lied to you, and that is fact, but the truth may be that she was planning a surprise

190

Reframing

birthday party for you and hiding details so she could ultimately bless you. When we are able to put what we see "in a different frame," our perspectives can be challenged and may not be as bad as what we thought they were. Facts improperly interpreted are not truth and lead to a lot of our hurt, anger, depression, anxiety, etc.

In order to properly reframe, we will have to know the frames that we have used in the past and be mindful that they will try to influence how we see things, maybe for the rest of our lives. Therapy and inner healing are crucial in gaining insight into these frames, labeling them, and learning how to reality test what we are seeing when our perceptions are framed with these antique, long-standing perspectives in our hearts. Those who have been hurt in the past (all of us), will be hypervigilant (a clinical term for hypersensitivity; it's like having our radar up all the time). This causes us to interpret our relationships as though we are constantly in danger of being hurt. Those of us who have been insecure in the past, for whatever reason, will be prone to constant negative self-talk and self-deprecating interpretations of what we see, putting ourselves down for the smallest mistakes. Take a minute to ask yourself and God what your faulty frames may be. This would be a good time to journal and let your heart experience the feelings behind all of those defenses. Letting yourself see and feel what is there does not have to invalidate your past wounds, but it can empower you to be protected from feeling like the past is reoccurring over and over in your life.

It's time to take the perceptions of our lives and "reframe" them like I did with the picture in my office. We may find that the pictures that look the worst aren't that way because of the artwork within them but because of the old, worn-out, battered frame that has been housing that piece of art. What look like the worst curses in our lives may actually be the biggest blessings when we look at them in their proper frame. God works through even the worst situations for our good (Romans 8:28), not because the situation is good and not even because He is making this "bad" thing happen, but He will bring lessons, truths, and new direction that will protect and guide us in new and better directions for years to come, even from the situations that hurt the most.

The Journey into the Divided Heart

It is our perceptions and interpretations of our negative circumstances that are the real culprits behind our depression and anxiety; they are much more than the hurtful and harmful events that we have endured. We can get all the inner healing we want, but without learning to reframe and perceive things correctly, we will be back in the same depression as before. You are, however, an overcomer! If you can find a way to take off the frames of the past and see the world around you more clearly and accurately, the world around you and the person inside of you may not be quite as bad as you presently perceive. Let's pray:

Father God, I understand more clearly today that, as Your Word says, I see in part and as through a glass dimly lit (1 Corinthians 13:12). My perceptions are skewed by my past, and I am prejudiced against anything that reminds me of my hurt and the wounds of the pasts. I ask You today to show me the frames that I perceive life through, that I might reframe how I see myself, others, and the situations and circumstances in my life. I ask to see things through Your eyes and to know how, by Your grace, to accurately discern what to do and how to react to my life on a daily basis. Even when the facts say that I am being hurt, show me the truth that You are right there with me. Even when the facts are that my circumstances are not ideal, show me that You have a plan for my life and my future that is good (Jeremiah 29:11). I ask for light where there is darkness so I can see what I do not see and know where my perceptions are skewed. I repent to You for interpreting and judging inaccurately because of my biases. Lead me to see things through Your eyes, I pray. Amen

It may be a good time to look at who else you need to repent to as well. You have likely judged others by the frames that have skewed your perceptions. Ask God to show you anyone you may have offended. Go to them today and say, "I was wrong. Will you forgive me?" Don't just say you're sorry; take responsibility by saying specifically, "I was wrong." There is freedom and hope available to you right now if you will give up your defenses.

Chapter 26: Setting Up Boundaries And Knocking Down Walls

Boundaries? Isn't that where you used to push people away from you to protect yourself? Isn't that where you learn to say "no" and cut most everyone out of your life? Aren't boundaries when you learn to be more assertive and stick up for yourself, thinking of yourself "for once" instead of putting everyone else first? Well, there is some truth to these assertions, but that's not really what a boundary is all about! A lot of boundary definitions sound like what I described back in the defense mechanism section and are not really boundaries at all. Boundaries and defenses are different, but they do have similar themes. Knowing the difference between the two is our next step—our next intervention! Many ministries and clinical settings move a person directly into boundary group therapy settings and seminars right after some inner healing and trauma work. That is how important boundary work really is! While we have found the need for boundary work also, I am putting this intervention before the section on inner healing and trauma because without some understanding of boundaries before going into the deep wounds of your heart, even your healing process could lead to further walls and perceived harm.

So let's talk about what a boundary really is. Think of a boundary as a property line between two houses. What does that property line do? Does it keep people out? Nope. Does it protect you? No, not really! Here is what it does do though: A property line divides precisely where responsibilities lie through establishing who owns what. Boundaries are all about responsibility. Boundaries are all about who is responsible for what, and in this they are meant to preserve and protect relationships, not destroy them like defenses and walls do. Isn't it nice that this line is marked out, surveyed, and in place before we even buy the lot? We can dispute where the line lies, but there is a record somewhere that defines the exact dividing line between our lot and our neighbor's.

That line, though invisible in many cases, tells us many things and makes our decision-making process much easier. That one little line does so much good! Many people either don't have a clue about what boundaries are or they avoid them like the plague because they think they will cause more conflict in their lives. Once defined and understood by both parties, though, boundaries do not do much to cause conflict; instead, they prevent it. Think about it. That property line tells us what part of the grass to cut and what part of the grass not to cut. That property line tells us where we can plant bushes and put up fences and where we cannot. That property line tells us how far we can let the leash out for the dog, and where the dog can do its business. And if, by chance, the dog crosses the line and uses the neighbor's side of the boundary line, who is responsible to clean it up? Not the neighbors. It's our job to go over and pick it up! Common courtesy even requires us to apologize to the neighbor for letting the dog be on their property. That line has saved us from arguing about such things and has effectively eliminated conflict in a number of categories. There's no question in the neighbor's mind about any of their responsibilities. Remember, boundaries are not like walls. They are not meant to protect us alone; boundaries protect relationship!

Anger is a red flag that we have a boundary that needs definition. There are all kinds of boundaries—emotional, physical, financial, spiritual, family structuring ones, and even some for self-care, just to name a few. Lack of boundaries in any of these areas will divide relationships rather than promote them. These boundaries need to be established to openly agree on things like what we are willing to share with others and what we are not. Boundaries will help define the expectations and roles within families and shouldn't change too fast or too often so the members of a family feel that life is predictable and consistent in the home. Boundaries are needed to define who pays for what financially. Business agreements and contracts are nothing more than documented boundaries. Even on a small financial scale, boundaries define who pays for lunch amongst friends. There are many more categories and examples, but I think you get the point. Boundaries need to be talked about, discerned, and defined as a means to protect our relationships and prevent conflict. Our old practice of not defining our boundaries well and using our defense mechanisms to cope with pain, thus distancing ourselves from others, needs to be discarded.

The property line example helps us see the most important aspect of boundaries. It is simple: *the property line is where we invite people onto our property and into our lives.* Boundaries can be as narrow or as broad as we choose to make them, but they will have a profound influence on how others relate to us. For example, if our boundaries are narrow and we invite the neighbors to cross our property line and visit our home, they will know that we like them. They will feel loved and accepted as we open our doors to them and ask them to come in. Boundaries are amazing tools to help people know how special they are to us. We use boundaries to build relationships with others. The problem is that socially we seldom know where the boundaries are, and we rarely engage in conversations that will bring us to a common understanding of where our boundaries lie. It is more often because we have no property lines that we end up experiencing certain cycles of conflict. There is a great deal more to learn about boundaries.

We all need Spirit-led boundaries. We tend to set up the wrong boundaries, but the Spirit of God is the master boundary setter. He is happy to direct us in our efforts when we ask Him in prayer.

Sometimes it is hard to tell when we are taking on too many responsibilities because our hearts want to help others. It is equally difficult to see when we are setting boundaries that are too narrow out of self-protection, our defense mechanisms, or even bitterness. Many of us believe we are loving others when we are actually enabling them—the result of skewed boundaries. Enabling means that we are making another person "able" to stay stuck where they are in a bad way. They are not becoming all that God called them to be, and we are not challenging them. Oftentimes we are more codependent than loving. This means we find our happiness in an unhealthy way by trying to make others happy. I have many parents in my office asking tough questions regarding whether or not they should kick their grown, non-working child out of the house. I have many husbands and wives of substances abusers asking how to handle their hungover spouse who wants them to call their boss and tell them that they are sick to excuse their absence. These are all difficult boundary situations. The way we handle these situations and others like them either teaches people that they are responsible for their own actions, or that we will step in and take responsibility for their actions for them. The first choice is a healthy one; the second is dysfunctional. The first choice lets another grow; the second allows them to be dependent on us to fix things for them.

What do you think the consequences will be if those we love learn inadvertently that there are no consequences to their actions? What do you think will happen if we take too much responsibility for them by paying for the costs of their failures over and over again? They will learn to continue in the same negative patterns they have found. Why? Because the best, and sometimes only, way we truly learn is from having to suffer the natural consequences of our actions. If we never learn to take responsibility for our own side of the property line, we are in danger of not being able to function properly in society. Spiritually, we are in even deeper trouble, as no one but ourselves will be answering for our decisions when we meet God on our judgment day. Setting boundaries that let others reap what they sow is truly loving them (Galatians 6:7), and we need help from the Holy Spirit to know when and how to set these lines.

The Holy Spirit will guide you through the process of setting up responsible and loving boundaries. It was for this purpose that I began the "Interventions" section with salvation, repentance, and why I taught about how to hear His still small voice. He will help you discern, and with the help of a good counselor, pastor, or discerning friend you will learn to rightly divide what your motives are in setting boundaries (1 Corinthians 4:5). This will help you to know when you are setting up walls and defenses instead of the boundaries that your relationships need. Remember the purpose of a defense mechanism or wall is to protect ourselves from perceived harm and to buffer us from emotional pain and hurt. A defense is most generally focused on us while a boundary takes others into account too. Boundaries consider the "us" and the "we," not just the "I." Walls are cold and controlling. Emotionally unhealthy people work overtime to keep their walls up. Boundaries actually show love and investment in the relationships that we have with others and are warm, even though it may feel tense when we are setting them up.

Here is the practical side of this. This is where you need to start with your own boundaries. I teach my Sunday school kids to step into the center of a plastic hoop to see what they are responsible for, so I will ask you to do the same. What is in the middle of the hoop when you step inside of it? You. Just you! Who is responsible for you? You are responsible for you! Everything inside of that hoop is yours, including your emotions, your thoughts, your physical body, your beliefs, your walls, your attitudes, your successes, and your failures. You are in control of these things and no one else! Everything outside of that hoop is not your responsibility until it is given to you directly and you agree to take ownership.

If others are working harder than you to make your life better, then you are not taking enough responsibility for your life. If you are striving and stressed and feel this process is going way too slow, then you may be taking too much responsibility, leading you too push too hard. If you are in need of housing, food, a job, medical care, transportation, and any other basic needs, it is your responsibility, within your boundaries, and on your side of the property line to get those needs met. Others may give you directions to the nearest shelter, tell you how to get disability, tell you about local churches to attend, but whose job is it to make those things happen? And who needs to take responsibility if it does not go well, and who gets the credit when it does? *You!* The good news is that if you invite Him, God is in the hoop too. He will guide and direct you. His Spirit-led boundary setting plan will balance your responsibilities His way!

In counseling and inner healing, we do as much as we can to define these boundaries, even by including consent forms that define the cost of treatment, the person's rights and responsibilities, and their job to attend sessions and follow through on agreed upon recommendations and tasks. When we don't understand that others (including our counselors) are supports and guides but that we are the responsible party, then things get messy. We need to understand that when we decide to truly pursue healing and our emotions get raw and grow in intensity, that it is not time to blame our support people. Instead, it's time to take responsibility and learn some new skills.

This same scenario happens with pastors, but it is often more difficult to define boundaries with our pastors and within our churches. Some churches get controlling because they try to take responsibility for the actions of those in their congregation. They try to become the Holy Spirit for them. This may sound harsh, but it's true. Other churches tend toward neglect of their congregation. This is usually done inadvertently because they don't understand, teach, discipline, and confront people as the Scripture says they should. Church leaders are in a position of authority; they are called to spur their people on to righteousness (Hebrews 10:24). Many church leaders do not understand that it is their responsibility to confront and discipline their people in love (Hebrews 12:6-10; 13:17) as a father would his kids. The boundaries between you and your pastor and your church need to be defined in light of your free-will choice. Only you can invite a leader into your life and allow yourself to be accountable to them.

Let's take an inventory right now. What boundary lines do you see that need to be defined and with whom? Is there anyone who is working harder than you at your healing and recovery? Is there any area that you are sitting back too much and looking for others to take responsibility when it is really an issue that is inside your hoop? Do you have conflict

Setting Up Boundaries And Knocking Down Walls

in relationships because you have not taken the time to discern and communicate about who is responsible for what and where the lines are? Maybe you can see that your anxiety is coming from some areas where you are taking too much responsibility, and it is time to let go. Maybe you can see that even between God and you, it is hard for you to tell what is His job and what is yours. Praying is great, but faith without deeds is dead (James 2:14-26), meaning that you still have to do your part. Or maybe you are the reverse of that and need to trust God more and act less. Letting your defenses down and understanding your responsibilities from others will allow for peace, joy, and love to come into your life. It will also establish parameters that will help you feel safe and allow you to fulfill your God-given need for companionship and true fellowship.

Let's pray and ask for help in this area, journaling anything that comes up as we pray:

Father God, I come to You in great need. Please help me to set and enforce healthy boundaries in my life. At times I feel walked over, and at times I feel stressed, showing that my boundaries need to be further defined and led by Your Holy Spirit. I am asking for Your Spirit to lead me into wisdom and insight so I can see the boundaries that need to be set in my life. Give me the courage and love that I need to set them effectively. Show me where my property lines are, O God, and anywhere that I am not taking enough responsibility in my life. Show me any areas of over-responsibility too, and free me from taking on what You have not given me to do. Your yoke is easy and Your burden is light (Matthew 11:30). I give up my defensiveness to You and decide today to focus on relationships rather than my own protection. Help me to hear and know the leading of Your Spirit as I move forward in lovingly communicating and defining these boundaries with those You have put in my life. Amen.

Chapter 27: Spiritual Warfare

Many people miss the true healing they seek because they don't understand that we live in two realms. We live in the physical realm, which is what we can see, touch, and taste, and we also live in the spiritual realm, which is the unseen. People get stuck in their disorders, lacking love, joy, and peace because they have been using interventions that are only medical. Some have been stuck in their disorders because they have been using interventions that are only based on emotional talk therapy; still others are stuck because they have been using interventions that are only religious. I may get in trouble with some counselors, doctors, and pastors with these statements, but healing is an all-inclusive process that requires an eclectic plan involving a multi-disciplined approach to all of the above areas that is led by prayer and the power of the Holy Spirit. Treating one third or two thirds of the whole person will not bring wholeness to anyone!

It is only when we realize that we are created as triune beings—made in the image of a triune God—that we will find the complete healing that we are looking for. Just as God is represented in three succinctly separate but fully one sovereign being (Father, Son, and Holy Spirit), we have three facets, which are listed in 1 Thessalonians 5:23 (among other places in Scripture) as our body, soul, and spirit. Our body is helped by looking at our medical needs, including our need for medications at times, our dietary needs, exercise, rest, and more. Our soul is our mind, our will, and our emotions; it needs to simply have someone to talk to, and it has feelings that we can validate and from which we gain insight and discernment. But thirdly, and most importantly, we need a plan for healing that also includes ministry spiritually.

This is definitely and by far the most neglected part of who we are. Most people have not had any ministry at the spiritual level and are not even sure what that looks like. Why? It is possible this spiritual level is neglected most because it is the level with which we are the least familiar. Unlike taking a pill or talking about our problems and receiving emotional support, the spiritual level requires us to sort through our beliefs about topics that we cannot prove with our natural eyes. The spiritual level requires us to have faith in some Being out there that is bigger than ourselves. Twelve-step programs call it a "higher power"!

After studying the defense mechanisms in this book, we can now see how much of the spiritual realm and the belief of its existence can be nullified by our defenses. In pursuing the spiritual realm, we can't intellectualize or rationalize as easily, and that makes many of us avoid this topic (another defense) because without a sense that our intellect is in control we feel very vulnerable and out of control. The truth is that we are *not* in control of anything, a fearful prospect to many, but finding out who *is* in control of the spiritual realm—our great God—will comfort and empower us, not scare us, in the end.

Now that you know you are a three-part being and understand that you find your identity in Christ Jesus when you are born again, let's explore spiritual warfare as an intervention. In the Bible, we find many passages that show us the realities of all that is happening behind the scenes in the unseen spirit realm, often unbeknownst to us as we live our lives day to day. The Bible gives us a behind-the-scenes look into the spiritual realm and all the main players on God's side versus Satan's side, as they each influence us invisibly. I want to paint a quick picture of the players listed in the Bible that make up the cast of the spiritual realm on the earthly stage.

God the Father, God the Son, God the Holy Spirit, and a multitude of angels populate one side of this unseen spiritual realm. There is also a figure named Satan on the other side. Just for the record, Satan is *not* the evil equivalent of God. There is no equivalent for God. He reigns supreme and sovereign. Satan is only a fallen angel (Luke 10:18) that has a hierarchy of evil spirits under him; their sole purpose is to *"steal and kill and destroy"* (John 10:10). Satan's group of fallen angels makes up his diabolical army, which opposes God's plans and especially hates God's favorite creation of all time—mankind. The good angels that did not follow Satan are God's *"ministering spirits"* (Hebrews 1:14), carrying out His commands and spreading God's good to all of us— even you! God and His angels are pitted against Satan and his demons in a great spiritual conflict between good and evil, and the focus of this conflict is us! Satan's plan is to destroy as many people as he can, while God who created us to be in relationship with Him resists the enemy's plans. You will be found on one of two sides—God's side with His amazing plan for your life or Satan's and his awful plan for your life.

How does Satan do this destroying? The Bible says that he is a liar (John 8:44); he is also called *"the accuser"* (Revelation 12:10). He accomplishes his work in non-Christians because they have not received a Savior yet. When Adam and Eve sinned way back in the garden of Eden, they gave their authority over the earth to Satan. Anyone who is not *born again* is living outside of God's authority just as Adam and Eve had to exist outside the garden after they sinned. But Satan doesn't give up trying to hurt us if we are Christians. He keeps lying and doing his best to destroy the good plans God has for His children. He is ruthless and full of hatred for us, after all, we are the apple of God's eye (Deuteronomy 32:10)! Satan will try to work through anything he can find, but he can only affect us when we give him authority in our lives by believing his lies. So lie he does! Even though we are threatened, the enemy is powerless to take that away from us. So he tries to make our lives here as miserable as possible instead.

While the Devil and his demons lie, harass, steal, and bombard us with everything evil at his disposal, the picture is not at all hopeless. We have not only God the Father, the Son, and the Holy Spirit on our side, but all the angels too, and they outnumber demons two to one (Revelation 12:4). The Bible also says there is a *"great cloud of witnesses"* that watch and intercede for us in this great battle (Hebrews 12:1). We have been given everything we need to fight in this spiritual war if we remain under the authority and protection of God as our loving Father. Scripture says that God has given us weapons (2 Corinthians10:4) and armor to protect us (Ephesians 6:10-18), with the added promise that we will be with Him and victorious in the end (1 Corinthians 15:57). Do you think that we come could ever gain true spiritual victory by using our little defense mechanisms and relying on our psychological walls? This spiritual battle is so much bigger than that, which is why our divided hearts so often lose out. We cannot rely on our own devices to stand and fight in this great battle with our puny little coping skills alone. As you study this in the Word of God, you will come to see that there really is an unseen war going on around us and inside of us, with many unseen players that are more powerful than we are. You will see the big picture.

As you gain understanding of spiritual warfare, you will be able to discern the truth from the lies of the enemy who wars against us, standing in God's protection against all that Satan is specifically attacking you with to thwart God's good plans. What does all of this have to do with therapy? If there is an unseen force led by Satan and he has lots of workers called demons helping him cause evil in us and in the whole earth and we do not address this issue in our healing process, then we are missing the very source and root of our symptoms!

I know this may get a little weird for some of you who are reading about it for the first time, so if taking a look at things spiritually is too much for your defense mechanisms right now, be assured that you can still get help to heal in the meantime as you sort out all of this spiritual stuff. The main point to this whole spiritual warfare teaching is that the "stinking thinking" that we experience can come in part from our own minds, but biblically those thoughts can also be attributed to Satan's lies, which makes them part of a spiritual battle too. The good news is that by standing under God's protection, simply not agreeing with the lies, and asking for God's truth in their place, these thoughts can easily be defeated and your peace preserved.

Spiritual Warfare

Understanding spiritual warfare means that you understand the truth that we *"do not wrestle against flesh and blood, but against principalities"* (Ephesians 6:12 NKJV). This means that our enemies are not other people! Your enemy is not your wife with whom you are angry. Your enemy is not your parent who didn't parent you correctly; it is not your kid who is driving you crazy; and it is not even your own self who you hate and despise most of the time. The enemy cannot be found in the natural realm, the realm of flesh and blood; instead, your enemy is in the spiritual realm where evil principalities dwell.

If we understand that people are not our enemy, we will be able to love them and accept them and forgive them when they do things wrong. This truth alone will help us tremendously in our counseling and healing process. People may still be responsible for their decision-making, but ultimately they were under the influence of a spiritual force that was empowering the circumstances that hurt us. We can let them off the hook by forgiving them and learn to fight God's way through spiritual warfare rather than fighting all of the loved ones who have hurt us.

The next step in understanding spiritual warfare is to understand who it is that we are fighting and how that battle is to be fought. The Bible has some specific passages that will help us recognize our enemy. You will find much of what it says familiar because the specific forces that we are coming against are all listed in the Bible in one form or another. The first step in any war is to know our enemy—get his name, rank, and serial number so we know the nature of how he fights and what weapons he uses. The Bible is specific about the different spirits we come up against in our war. These spirits are named according to their function, describing what they do specifically. The Bible talks about a spirit of fear (2 Timothy 1:7), a spirit of heaviness or depression (Isaiah 61:3), a spirit of infirmity or sickness (Luke 13:10-17), lying spirits (1 Kings 22:21-23), a seducing spirit (1 Timothy 4:1), a spirit of disobedience (Ephesians 2:2), a spirit of bondage (Romans 11:15), and a deaf and dumb spirit (Mark 9:25), just to name a few. So much of what we deal with emotionally can be put into these categories. You can study up on each of these and more—just open your Bible!

The Journey into the Divided Heart

The Bible urges us not to be ignorant of the schemes of the enemy. It is more important to be aware of these schemes than be able to name each demon or stronghold we are up against in the spiritual realm. In other words, learn what it is that Satan is trying to do, and what plays are in the playbook he keeps calling against you? Did you know one of the most popular plays in his playbook is to get us offended? That's right, and that play scores him a touchdown with many of us all the time. Why would he want to get us offended? He uses this scheme because the Bible says, *"Don't let the sun go down while you are still angry, for anger gives a foothold to the devil"* (Ephesians 4:26 NLT). This open door is often unforgiveness—the sun went down and we did not forgive and release others from our right to punish them. This feeds into using anger as a defense mechanism. The Greek word for offense is *skandalon* and means "entrapment" (Luke 17:1). A *skandalon,* or offense, is a trap. Like the little bar on the mouse trap that holds the cheese, any area of offense leads to our spiritual demise. What bait leads you to be caught in the trap of offense?

There are many other schemes, and I will name a few more, but the main point is that when we recognize that we are in a spiritual war and that people are not our true enemy, we will commit our issues to God in prayer rather than fighting with people. The Bible says that the enemy wants to divide households. Any of you going through that? Have you prayed? Have you waged war spiritually? The Bible says that a house divided against itself cannot stand and that Satan comes like a roaring lion trying to divide his prey from the pack (Mark 3:25; 1 Peter 5:8).

How do we fight a spiritual war? First, do not be afraid! Don't get spooked; this does not have to get weird. We don't want be focused on the enemy, the demons, or any of his schemes more than we are on Jesus. Jesus said that He is *"the way and the truth and the life"* (John 14:6). The Bible say that all authority was given to Him under heaven (Matthew 28:18). Jesus made a spectacle of Satan and triumphed over him at the cross (Colossians 2:15). Jesus spoke and the Devil fled (James 4:7), and this is still the case today. Most of the deliverance process (being set free spiritually) has to do with recognizing that there is real spiritual warfare in addition to following the steps listed previously—salvation, repentance, reframing, establishing your boundaries by engaging our free will toward Him, and declaring the name of Jesus in prayer.

Scripture says that what we bind on earth is bound in the heavens, and so we pray, asking our Father God in the name of Jesus to bind the enemy, naming his schemes when we can and rendering him powerless in our lives. You can try it right now. Pray, but even more, **declare** this aloud, by saying *"I recognize that a spirit of (fear, depression, sickness, mental illness, (fill-in-the-blank) is at work in my life, and right now in the name of Jesus Christ of Nazareth, I bind it from having influence or authority in my life according to what Jesus taught in Matthew 18:18."*

Even some pastors have not been taught some of the basics principles of spiritual warfare. I remember having a pastor in my office once who prayed this way for the first time with tremendous results. I remember that he felt attacked from some people in his church. After learning to "bind" the spirit of accusation, he felt such relief afterward that he slept for the first time in weeks. I also remember the pastor who came to my office certain he should leave the ministry because he had lustful thoughts about women when he got behind the pulpit to preach. He learned to pray in his mind, *I bind a spirit of lust in Jesus' name.* Immediately he experienced the freedom to preach his sermon without feeling the shame the enemy was trying to heap on him. I know many who have learned to do this in the middle of all kinds of conflict—between family members, in marriages, between friends. *"Father God, I bind any spirit that is bringing division right now."* They have also learned how to pray using the second half of that Scripture which says, *"Whatever you loose on earth will be loosed in heaven."* Heaven is full of love, joy, and peace, and in prayer you can receive this all into your hearts and households today. You can pray, *"Loose Your love in this household, in Jesus' name."* Pray and watch the atmosphere in your emotions, your thoughts, your relationships, and your households change! The Bible says that if by the Spirit of God the enemy is bound and driven out, then *"the kingdom of God* [including His love, peace, and joy] *has come upon you"* (Matthew 12:28).

The Journey into the Divided Heart

For the believer, spiritual warfare is a matter of believing Luke 10:19: "*I have given you authority to trample on snakes and scorpions and to overcome all the power of the enemy; nothing will harm you.*" For the unbeliever, it is time for you to recognize that you need a higher power to fight and win this battle between good and evil that you are in. Learn to command the enemy to go and leave you alone, stopping the thoughts that threaten you by speaking to God and to yourself in prayer, "*I come out of agreement with any thought right now that is not from God in Jesus' name.*" Admit the thought and, as a prayer of repentance, decide what you will believe and pray like this, for instance: "*I come out of agreement with this thought that I am a failure and command it to go in Jesus' name.*" You can pray aloud that "*any evil spirit here within the sound of my voice has to leave in Jesus' name.*" The prayer of faith, declared in the authority that Jesus gave you by what He did on the cross, will bring change to your body, soul, and spirit.

As you pray and practice fighting your thoughts and anything else that does not line up with the good and perfect plan God has for your life, be sure to note the changes that happen thereafter. They may feel subtle and small to you at first. After you pray and make a declaration of personal well-being, be mindful of what you feel, what you are thinking, how your body is reacting, and how your level of peace has increased. Many times after you pray like this, you will notice an immediate change in your peace and joy; additionally, you will sense a change in your heart. A soft, undivided heart of love will become more evident to you. Sometimes you will feel increased symptoms of anger, fear, and distractions too. They don't call it spiritual warfare for nothing! Don't be alarmed. The battle may also increase some when you pray this way! It is not out of the ordinary to feel the healing power of God immediately as we pray either. This may come in the form of a physically warm feeling, tingly vibrations, even feelings of electricity. God is in the healing business, so don't forget to recognize and thank Him as He touches your body, your emotions, your wounds, your soul, and your spirit too! He is a good God.

Spiritual Warfare

Let's pray and do a little spiritual warfare together right now, out loud if you can.

Dear Heavenly Father, I come to You right now believing that there is a spiritual war in and around me, and I am asking for Your help. I believe there is a God and there is also a Satan. I believe there is not only a realm I can see but a realm I cannot. I believe, God, that my struggle is not against flesh and blood, but as Your Word says it is against principalities and the powers of wickedness from Satan. I am sorry and repent for fighting against people as if they were my enemy and for not recognizing that there are forces from Satan and his army that are working against Your good plans in my life. I see the work of fear and heaviness, mental illness, physical infirmity, offenses, and division in many areas of my life. I believe You are more powerful than any of these workings of Your enemy, Satan, and I come to ask You for help. I declare as Your Word teaches us that I have authority over anything that would harm me because of what You did for me on the cross. As You taught us in Matthew 18:18, I bind any and all spirits of fear, anxiety, depression, mental illness, infirmity, and all demonic influences from having authority in my life in the powerful name of Jesus Christ of Nazareth. I say to these spirits and all others within the sound of my voice to go right now in Jesus' name. I receive in place of these things a fresh new filling of all that is in Your kingdom including love, joy, peace, and healing on all levels. Fill me with Your Holy Spirit in every part within me. I receive Your love, Your healing, and deliverance right now and I thank You for it in Jesus' name. Amen.

Now hold out your hands and receive and notice what you feel, what you see, what you sense, and what your body is feeling. Be sure to journal what just happened.

Chapter 28: Inner Healing

Inner healing is just what it sounds like—healing on the inside—but it is a healing of emotions, a healing of the soul, and the spirit! I hope you see, as I have come to see, that there is a big difference between doing some counseling and talking through our problems and an actual inner *healing*! I remember coming out of school for social work feeling as though I were ready to take on the world those many years ago. It did not take long to see the revolving door in the counseling agencies where I worked and come face to face with professional discouragement instead. I remember stepping back and saying, "Is this really what I want to do?" It began to feel like we were putting bandages on gaping wounds—leaving people's hearts divided internally. How long would a doctor last in a practice if he saw nobody cured? I was not going to last long as a counselor if I did not see healings, I knew that for sure.

I was a hungry young soul though, always searching for more. I loved my clients so much that there was nowhere I would not travel to learn and grow and bring back tools for my counseling toolbox. The goal was nothing less than the absolute healings I saw in the Bible, where the lame walked, the blind saw, and deaf regained their hearing. I had even read that the dead were raised! My field, my giftings, and my focus were on the broken and divided heart, though. So I questioned: How did this healing happen on an emotional level? What did it look like?

I remember preparing for a retreat for my small home group and preaching that week on what God was showing me about healing. A pastor friend of mine said, "Steve, you are preaching Theophostic

211

Ministry." I said, "*Theo*—what?" He said there was a prayer ministry that taught what I was teaching called Theophostic Ministry. In time, I learned there were dozens of inner healing prayer models springing up in the church community, and that this was just one of them. Theophostic is composed of two Greek words: *theo* meaning "God's" and *phos* meaning "light."[8] Their prayer ministry tool was teaching people the specifics that I did not have. They taught how to get out of the way and let the Holy Spirit do the counseling His way, which brought true and miraculous change!

After learning this tool with my pastor and friends, testing it scripturally, and deciding to take the R-I-S-K (yes, I had my fish bowls too), I began to practice. Guinea pig number one came into my office feeling pretty good, saying that she thought she had been given some great insights in our three sessions focusing on her marriage and that she thought she was finished after this. With forty-five minutes left in our session, I asked for permission to try a new way of counseling. She trusted me and said yes. I explained to her, as I will to you now, that inner healing prayer is led by God, not by a counselor's line of questioning. In prayer we simply ask God to shine His light, giving His revelation to areas in our divided hearts that are not peaceful and whole. I prayed a general prayer with no specific leading, "*Father God, would You please shine Your light on any area of her heart that You would like to heal today.*" A little nervous myself, I looked up after thirty seconds or so to find my client in a complete panic attack! This sent my divided heart into its own defense mechanisms! I wanted to let God work, but my mind screamed that things seemed to be worse after I prayed. (I needed reframing!)

Long story short, when given the opportunity in prayer like this, I have found God to so often go to that deepest wound, the place that is still dark and troubled in a person's heart. He wanted to heal her, and heal her He did! She re-experienced a memory from long ago of having an abortion. (Be aware of your defenses right now if you have had

8. Smith, Ed M. *Theophostic Ministry* (Advanced Training Series Level Two, Dissociation and Trauma Based Mind Control). Campbellsville, KY: New Creation Publishing, 2002.

similar pain, and stay with me; maybe God wants to heal you too!) The cognitive distortions of her stored trauma were all shame-based, and she screamed, "I murdered my child, and I should never be forgiven."

In secular CBT counseling, we would have tried to rationalize this shame away and challenge her self-abasing thoughts. In the church, we would, of course, pray with her and lead her toward asking forgiveness for her shame and then forgiving herself and letting the shame go. In inner healing, though, we just repeat what the client gives us, and we offer their emotions and thoughts up to Jesus for Him to reframe and speak truth into. If you have ever had a moment of inner healing like this, then you will know what I am talking about. For the rest of you, I wish my words were not so inadequate. It is hard to describe the power and miraculous change that occurred. My client had a vision of Jesus being with her in that room. (He is in all places at all times, see Jeremiah 23:24.) Jesus spoke to her, reassuring her of His tender love and total acceptance of her. She felt His touch as real as if I had touched her. He let her into His heart of compassion and sadness for what she went through. I could see and feel her whole insides change! Her divided heart found complete relief. The part of her that hated herself and needed to be in control to make sure she would never fail like this again was ministered to, and in an instant she was changed.

If you ask her today, as I have, she would tell you that she still knows she is forgiven and that she is loved by God, which makes it easy for her to love herself. She was completely healed! Healing is miraculous! It accomplishes a goal that no human could accomplish in themselves! The traumatized place inside her became a place of peace and calm because Jesus made it so. I could have said the same things He did but with minimal effect. Her healing came from her Creator and she knew it! These results are mirrored in Scripture when Jesus spoke to the storm, saying, *Peace, be still!* (Mark 4:39 NKJV). The turbulent seas instantly went calm! Jesus holds the key to every heart, yours and mine. That day He spoke to the storm inside of her divided heart, and those traumatic, stormy places inside became calm.

The Journey into the Divided Heart

This is what I want for your life too. More importantly, this is what God wants for your life! You can imagine that the healing of this trauma and replacing those shame-based thoughts with love deep down inside her soul led to an amazing, yet natural, change in her emotions and then in her behaviors. Though you may not have had an abortion or been sexually abused, there are places that are emotionally bruised inside you, too. They are sensitive to the touch. You feel you need your defenses. Perhaps you even need to dissociate because the pain is still excruciating there. Inner healing is the true intervention that will take you to the root of that pain and heal it.

I could share hundreds of stories and testimonies. I could contrast this level of inner healing to secular CBT by itself and show you how trauma work that used to take years can yield much better results in only weeks through prayer. I could share how many use this type of intervention on themselves whenever they are stirred up and emotionally charged. This ministry has raised the bar for me, and it can never be lowered. I will always meet people right where they are, never pressure them, and respect their beliefs wholeheartedly, no matter who they are and where they are in their recovery. However, I can never stop hoping that their sessions will be like that of the client I just related to you, and that in an instant their broken heart will receive the peace that my other clients receive.

There are many different inner healing models today; many of them have great value and give specialization to different areas of ministry in the Christian Church today. However, as you will see here, many have the same themes and similar components, just using different words and concepts. "Sozo" prayer ministry is another that is used by Bethel Church in California, written by De Silva and Liebscher. *Sozo* is the Greek word translated "saved, healed, delivered." Sozo ministry is a unique inner healing and deliverance ministry aimed to get to the root of things hindering your personal connection with the Father, Son, and Holy Spirit. With a healed connection, you can walk in the destiny to which you have been called. You can see how similar this sounds to Theophostic, but it uses some different "tools" to get to the roots of your problems. There are six main tools that the Sozo team uses:

- Father Ladder
- Four Doors
- Presenting Jesus
- The Wall
- Trigger Mechanisms (advanced tool)
- Divine Editing (advanced tool)

A Sozo session is a time for a Sozo prayer minister to sit down with you and with the help of the Holy Spirit walk you through the process of freedom and wholeness. Sozo is not so much a counseling session but a time of interacting with Father, Son, and Holy Spirit for wholeness and pursuing of your destiny. Their tools aim at forgiveness, seeing things through Jesus's eyes, identifying walls (like defense mechanisms), and the "presenting Jesus" tool which asks Jesus in prayer to come into places of the heart that are still traumatized and filled with pain. Sozo also has a component of working with dissociation called *shabar*, which is a Hebrew word meaning "broken-hearted" from Isaiah 61:1.

Sozo connects you with the trinity and allows Him to take you to any roots of your emotional and behavioral symptoms, with a unique focus on the need to choose immediately to forgive all, and with the similarities to other models that it acknowledges only God as the healer and the director to any areas of hidden woundedness that need to be addressed.

Lastly, my personal favorite of late is called HeartSynch led by Reverend Andrew Miller. As inner healing models have grown and evolved over the last couple decades, they have kept the theme of getting to our root issues by the guidance of the Holy Spirit through prayer. Much has been learned through the years, however, and Rev. Miller has added some key elements to this inner healing model that makes it stand apart. First, HeartSynch will begin all sessions with a covering prayer and what is called a "five-bar moment" (like a cell phone fully connected to the tower) where we ask the Holy Spirit to show you a time when you have felt really close to God. This Immanuel moment can be a life-changing time whereby you experience the closeness of attachment with God, a safe place, home base, from which to heal any place that your heart is hurting. Rev. Miler uses neurology to help explain that we all have "core parts" in the way our mind is created with a left brain from which we "function" logically mostly, a right brain from which we experience "emotion" and relationship, and the amygdala (mentioned previously as our fight or flight center) where we "guard(ian)" our hearts. It is refreshing to see this model focus us wholly on needing peace in our emotions, understanding of how to protect ourselves without all the defense mechanisms listed previously, and also on functioning in our daily lives at the level we are destined. Loving "the Lord our God with all our heart, all our strength, and all our mind" (Luke 10:27) comes from having these core areas of ourselves peacefully connected to each other and to God. It is a beautiful thing to experience!

The following components of HeartSynch make it able to address most of what has been mentioned in this book previously. Rev. Miler deals with spiritual warfare by simply praying from Zechariah 3:2 (and in Jude 1:9) where He says: "The Lord rebuke you, Satan! The Lord, who has chosen Jerusalem [and choses you and me], rebuke you!"

HeartSynch even gives tools to bring peace to the attachment level pain that is pre-verbal and largely subcortical (subconscious and involuntary). Dissociation is dealt with from the most subtle to the most severe levels, with the understanding that we all become "desynchronized" in our day-to-day walks and that connecting to God and self through this type of prayer in our emotions, our logic, and our neurological place of defending ourselves not only leads us to peace but teaches us the means to stay in that peace in our daily lives.

With their permission, I have shared the websites and contact information of each of these three ministries at the end pages of this book. Please contact them for further help and training. There are many clinical settings, such as ours at Renewal Christian Counseling Centers, and many Christian churches and community programs that use these inner healing models as they minister to and help people. Seek them out and find an "inner healing" that may be the missing link in becoming emotionally whole. As you decide to leave the "Skippy" fish bowl and any comfort zones you may have had to pursue all that God has for you, please don't stop at just getting your own inner healing. Get trained to pray others through their pain also. The divided heart is made whole as it receives ministry and then freely gives to others (Matthew 10:8)! As you will find in learning these inner healing tools, your inner healing can happen anytime and at any place though. Let's pray right now and see what the Lord might want to show you as you pray the following inner healing prayer. You might want to take out a pen and paper and note all that comes up while you sit for a minute and ponder after you pray.

Dear Lord Jesus, I come to You today hearing that You heal us on the inside and knowing that there are likely deep places inside of me that hold unresolved pain and trauma too. The bar has been raised for me here today, and I don't want to just cope with my pain with my own defense mechanisms any longer. I want You to heal it! So I am asking You now to shine Your light on any place inside of me that You would like me to go. I choose to embrace whatever feelings I need to feel and remember whatever it is I need to remember. Shine Your light on the roots of my symptoms, show me where You were then, and replace any of my perspectives with Yours. Bring to me what no counselor on their own could ever bring—the truth that calms even the greatest storms inside me. I choose to let You lead me wherever You want to go and to receive whatever You want to show me, in Jesus' name. Amen!

Chapter 29: Gaining Attachments

You were hardwired to *need* more than acquaintances; you were built to *need* real attachments! This intervention has everything to do with getting you past your divided heart and living from your God-given, spiritually and genetically programmed *need* for attached relationships. Be sure to track your defenses on this one too. They will be on high alert against this emotionally vulnerable way of living, as it will lead you to live with an exposed and open heart to others!

Psychology has only been studying attachment for about sixty to seventy years. Lately, they have focused increasingly on what attachment is and how the human brain functions relationally and emotionally. The church has not given much attention to attachment either—not from behind the pulpit or in their emotional healing models. The superficial, behavioral changes that the church in general is pursuing neglect a lot of the neurological levels of our minds that need to be renewed, so we need to keep learning and growing in this clinically as well as in the church community. Learning a little about attachment theory and the neurology of your brain will help you tremendously in your journey. Attachment theory is a neurological explanation of why we act, choose, and feel the way we do. It is fascinating to see how our brains were *"fearfully and wonderfully made"* by our Creator (Psalms 139:14). Seeing healing through the lens of attachment and neurology will give you a road map to keep you from getting lost in the process.

Neurologists have mapped out five basic levels of our brain that we need to understand first to direct our healing process toward the attachment level. Here is a brief synopsis of these levels and some basic facts that we need to know about each of them. Special thanks to Friesen, Wilder, Bierling, Koepcke, and Poole from Shepherd's House Ministry for their amazing work on the parts of our brain in these five levels. For a more thorough study, get their book *The Life Model: Living from the Heart Jesus Gave You*.[9] Each section in italics that follows is part of their 5 Level Processing Model as described by Dr. Karl Lehman and Charlotte E. T. Lehman.

Level 1: Thalamus

> *"Level 1: Level 1 contains the neurological circuitry that moderates attachment (bonding) to other people. At any given moment, activity in your level 1 circuits determines whether you are operating from a foundation of secure attachment, dismissive attachment, distracted attachment, or disorganized attachment. Level 1 attachment circuits also initiate the emotional experience of joy when we perceive that someone is glad to be with us."* [10]

The thalamus is the attachment center of the brain and has traditionally not been targeted for healing by counselors or pastors. Nevertheless, it is at the core of everything we feel, think, and do. The thalamus is located at the brain stem toward the back of the brain. Thalamus level processing controls memory, alertness, and consciousness; it also defines and labels who is personable and friendly to us.

---

9. Friesen, James G., E. James Wilder, Anne M. Bierling, Rick Koepcke, and Maribeth Poole. *The Life Model: Living from the Heart Jesus Gave You*. Shepherds House, 1999.

10. Lehman, Karl D. M.D. and Charlotte E.T. Lehman, M.Div. "Brain Science, Psychological Trauma, and the God Who Is with Us, Part II: The Processing Pathway for Painful Experiences 1 and the Definition of Psychological Trauma." K.D. Lehman MD. Revised 2/4/2011. 8-9.

Gaining Attachments

Our thalamus, or our brain stem, is primitive and is programmed from the very beginning of our lives through eye-to-eye contact with a primary caregiver, synchronizing energy levels for over eight hours a day growing neuropathways, especially during the first twelve months of life. These pathways become our "internal interpreter" of the world around us for the rest of our lives. This internal interpreter, if programmed by attachment figures who are attentive, emotionally stable, present, available, and calming, will forever define our world at some level, as safe, loving, and secure. If we were raised in a home where there was not a secure base, though, our thalamus will be programmed to define our world as unsafe, unloving, and insecure at a foundational level. Unconscious to us, our brain will consistently tell us that something is wrong if the thalamus was programmed with even the smallest attachment wound early on. A healthily trained thalamus will register a belief that others are glad to see us, which E. James Wilder and his colleagues define as "joy." If we were not synchronized with a secure attachment figure early in life, our thalamus will forever register a level of shame which *The Life Model* defines as the opposite of joy. In essence, we will consistently think that others are not glad to see us.

When there is a void or a wound in the thalamus, we often feel an intense absence of joy, having no real contentment or sense of security inside. Thalamus level pain leaves us without joy, resulting in a sort of deep-down, nagging ache, the kind of ache that never really goes away. Some say attachment pain is the most painful pain that a human being can ever have, which is why this section is so important for us to know about.

Level 2: Amygdala

"Level 2: Level 2 contains the neurological circuitry that moderates connection to an experience. If an experience moderately exceeds our involuntary capacity, one set of level 2 neurological mechanisms cause emotional disconnection. If an experience more severely exceeds our involuntary capacity, a second set of level 2 neurological mechanisms cause complete dissociative disconnection by routing the content

The Journey into the Divided Heart

through an alternative processing pathway. When this happens the experience is completely disconnected from our normal conscious awareness and from our conscious autobiographical memory."

The amygdala is the part of the brain that controls our hardwired fight, flight, or freeze center created to keep us alive in the midst of biological threats. The amygdala controls our survival instinct and also operates on a very primitive, black-and-white basis—it registers everything in our world as good or bad, safe or unsafe. The amygdala is not concerned with relationship. This makes it impossible to connect with people or God when it is activated. The panicky feeling experienced at level two in the brain can be real or imagined, but either way, it will bring the same feelings of being out of control and with it the drive to preserve self. The amygdala, when activated, uses our autonomic nervous system to prepare us for self-defense through either fight, flight, or freeze. This part of our brain has everything to do with our defense mechanisms; it's important to be able to tell when we are operating from this level 2 processing.

The amygdala can become overactive and lead us into a hypersensitive, hypervigilant state of always being in a fight or flight mode. The amygdala doesn't use logic to determine the realities of its safety; that would take too much time. The amygdala relies on associations or memories of past events to determine whether we are safe. An overactive and unbalanced amygdala leaves us in perpetual tension and anxiety!

Diane Hawkins from Restoration in Christ Ministries affectionately addresses the people who are processing out of our amygdala as "Amy." [11]Sometime it helps to call out our amygdala, to know wew are processing from this part of our brain so we can at least question whether our fear is logical or not. Often our amygdala is heightened to a level of processing that attachment experts call "amygdala hijacking." When this happens, a person's thinking is dominated by the survival

11. Diane Hawkins, *Multiple Identities* (Grottoes, VA: Restoration in Christ Ministries, 2009), 80-82.

222

instinct located in this part of the brain. Ask this part of your brain, "How are you doing, Amy?"

Level 3: Cingulate Cortex

"Level 3 contains the neurological circuitry that moderates relational connection to others. The level 3 right-sided cingulate cortex is the part of our brain that our mind uses to maintain attuned relational connection to the Lord and/or others in our community, even during painful experiences; and when we experience a negative emotion that is beyond the ability of our level 3 skills, and we therefore temporarily become non-relational and lose joy; the level 3 cingulate cortex is the part of our brain that our mind uses to re-establish attuned relational connection. For those of you familiar with Dr. Wilder's teaching, this is where "returning to joy" comes in, because once our level 3 circuits have reestablished attuned relational connections, our level 1 attachment circuits reestablish joy."

Level 3 is called our cingulate cortex. It registers joy and relationships and does so by tracking the non-verbal messages of others and telling our prefrontal cortex that we are connected to others. Its purpose is to register extreme joy and contentment when this connection is present. Our cingulate cortex is a busy part of our brain, constantly interpreting our world for us by tracking others at an the incredible cycle speed of five times a second, telling us, based primarily on eye contact with others, whether we are in "sync" with them or not. The cingulate cortex registers feelings of connectedness, bringing contentment to us as God has ordained. But if this part of our brain has not had opportunity to develop the ability to stay in or return to joy, it will not easily recognize when we are having these moments of intimacy and contentment. We could be being loved by others and not know it, as it would not register in our cingulate cortex.

The Journey into the Divided Heart

Like working out a muscle, the cingulate cortex needs to be pushed and developed in order to build a capacity to recognize and fully experience intimate relationship and joy. Working out our cingulate cortex to build joy and capacity for intimacy will not be possible until "Amy" lets her guard down. The testimony of having even one new trusting relationship can reprogram our brain to feel that it has obtained the intimacy that it has been programmed to need. The world tries to build intimacy and relational capacity through sex and common interests, but the cingulate cortex knows (even if other parts of our brain do not) when it is just being used and when the love of another is fake or shallow. There is no substitute to this part of our brain for true relationship and intimacy! God created us for intimacy with Himself and others, and this is the place in the brain that is created to feel and experience it!

Levels 4 and Level 5: Prefrontal Cortex and Left Prefrontal Cortex

"Level 4: Level 4 contains the neurological circuitry that helps us hold on to our true hearts as the source of discernment and choices, even when we are dealing with difficult situations.... The level 4 right prefrontal cortex is the part of the brain that the mind uses to discern, "How do I handle this situation? How can I navigate this situation in a way that I will be satisfied with after it's all over?" Level 4 also contains the neurological circuitry that calms the brain down—after the source of distress has been resolved, these level 4 circuits take the brain from the subjective experience of feeling negative emotions to the subjective experience of feeling peaceful/calm.

Level 5: Level 5 contains the neurological circuitry that helps us "make sense" out of our experiences and interpret the meaning of our experiences. The level 5 left prefrontal cortex is the logical, analytical, linguistic part of the brain that the mind uses to come up with explanations, models, paradigms, and worldviews. The level 5 prefrontal cortex is the part of the brain that the mind uses to build an autobiographical narrative that tells the story of our experience."

There is so much more to share on these levels. These are the parts of our brain that hold our higher functioning abilities—reason, emotions and emotional regulation, judgment, and logic. Our prefrontal cortex is what distinguishes us from the animal kingdom and gives us our God-given ability to sense, feel, think, reason, and discern. Unfortunately, not many of us are using our "thinker" these days! The prefrontal cortex grows and develops properly when in a secure attachment, and as attachment theorists say, "Neurons that fire together wire together."

When the thalamus has attachment wounds, the amygdala is overactive and on high alert. Subsequently, the cingulate cortex does not know how to register joy, and the prefrontal cortex does not "fire" together with the other levels, leaving our brains unregulated and, at times, out of our control. The prefrontal cortex coordinates and manages all the levels of the brain. It can synchronize the emotions (right prefrontal) and thoughts and logic (left prefrontal) along with the other lower three levels of brain functioning to lead a balanced, healthy, and whole life.

The prefrontal cortex is called the "identity center" by Wilder. When it has had opportunity to grow dendrites and neuropathways appropriately within a safe attached environment, it is able to maintain a secure sense of "who I am" even in the midst of emotional pain. The goal of attachments is for all the levels of the brain to hold a healthy and whole positive sense of self that then becomes the secure foundation (especially when backed with a knowledge of God's Word) from which to function, learn, and grow. The prefrontal cortex oversees these efforts when we put it to work coordinating all the levels. Knowing these levels will help us target the neurological root of our emotional symptoms, helping us to know more precisely where to invite the healing work of our Father in heaven.

INVENTORY TIME

This is a good time to stop and take inventory of the levels of your brain, really looking at how each of these sides is functioning, as well as how each of these sides of you has been programmed. Has your thalamus been programmed to be at ease because it knows it has had a safe haven and a set of foundational attachments from which to feel secure and unconditionally loved? Has your amygdala been at ease, waiting for real threats, or is it on constant high alert, causing hypervigilance and anxiety? Is your cingulate cortex registering joy and intimacy, connecting and synchronizing to others consistently using eye contact? Has your prefrontal cortex been able to reason and discern what is happening, not reacting to the triggers around you but discerning from your true identity, as Dr. Wilder says: "Knowing who I am, and what it's like me to do in this situation"?

So many times people have been in therapy for years, and have felt that some progress was made, but just sensed that something was missing. So many times, clinicians have known to give support, refer for medications, do some good cognitive behavioral therapy, and maybe even do some inner healing, but if we do not understand these five levels of the brain, then we will not be able to track what is fully needed for us and our clients to be whole emotionally as God intended. Dr. Wilder's five levels of the brain call us to focus on all the levels of the brain and intervene as deeply as possible, knowing that the positive results of deeper levels healing will automatically benefit the higher-level functions of the person.

Most therapies will focus on levels 4 and 5, using talk therapy to rationally address the left brain and reasoning centers of the brain alone. These cognitive based therapies can be highly effective until someone is triggered or stirred up emotionally on the lower levels, at which time their level 4 and 5 functioning usually go offline. Some, but much fewer, therapies have focused on helping people to build relationship capacity, emotional regulation tools, and knowing how to synchronize with others on level three, but more attention in therapy and inner healing needs to be given to this and the lower levels of our brain. This is what Dr. Wilder's five levels teaching is bringing to light. Level three emotional pain is hard enough to access, and most clinicians have had minimal training on how to address such intense pain. With training on how to intervene on these levels of the brain, though, interventions can be given to address the presence of deeper-level pain and woundedness. It is in addressing the lower-level brain functioning that interventions can be given to rewire our guardian and attachment level places of protection to be whole and fully peaceful.

Maybe you have been in church, in ministry, and/or in counseling for some time, and you know that you have had some intense attachment wounding and struggle with feeling secure and consistently belonging. Maybe your level-two amygdala is always activated, causing emotional and then resulting physical problems, which have never been resolved. Take time to assess the levels of your brain and know what you are asking God and others for and at what levels you struggle the most.

DEFINING ATTACHMENT

When I first started asking God for revelation on attachments, the first definition that I received was that an attachment relationship is one that operates in a "permanence of love"! Permanence of love? Some of you may be saying from your hopelessness, "Is there any such thing as permanent love in this world?" Attachment is forever—from the cradle to the grave! In the framework of most who have attachment issues, though, the only certainty they have experienced in life is death and taxes; they have not had many, if any, relationships in their lives that have been a safe haven that reflected the permanence of love. They unconsciously look to their thalamus, finding no sufficient database of others who have been permanently loving to them; then they go to their "Amy" (the amygdala) and find lots of reasons for fight or flight from the obvious dangers of intimacy. It doesn't help that they have very few, if any, testimonies in their cingulate cortex to register the joy and contentment of intimacy. The permanence of love is not even logical to them on a prefrontal cortex level; they reason that some have loved, but all have betrayed them at one level or another in their lives. (Betrayal is a huge attachment term!)

The Journey into the Divided Heart

If attachments scare you, it is because of your divided and highly defended heart! To be quite honest, your defense mechanisms have a good point in trying to protect you. There *is* emotional danger inherent to attachments because, by definition, separation at any level from a true attachment *will* bring pain! That's right! Emotional pain is by definition a part of having true attachments! This guarantee of pain and other key aspects of attachments were defined by John Bowlby back in the 1950s, and are listed below. The list is in bold; the explanation is mine.

1. Attached relationships seek closeness in times of trouble.

A person in an attached relationship will, by instinct and reflex, naturally pursue being close to those they are in attachments with in times of difficulty. Just like a baby cries when upset, hungry, or in need of a diaper change, we automatically reach out for those who are our foundational supports, unless our hearts are divided and defended.

2. Attachments are a safe haven.

Attachments have everything to do with safety and where and with whom we feel safe. When we feel safe, we are the goofiest, nerdiest, most uninhibited version of ourselves ever. We try to hide this part of ourselves often, as there is great vulnerability in sharing from this safe place. Safety equals not being protective and guarded. An attachment relationship becomes that place where we can be our truest self because we know we are always loved!

3. Exploration takes risks.

A toddler in an attached relationship with mom and dad will take his first steps on time developmentally because he has that safe haven and that home base from which to explore and take risks. He can always turn around and, through eye contact alone, experience the security of knowing that help and protection is right there, willing and able. This type of security makes it easier to move outside of our comfort zones and take the risks that lead to growth. The healthy, attached person is not overcome by anxiety in uncharted territory but takes confident steps in exploring the unknown.

4. Separation brings anxiety and anger.

As mentioned before, inherent to attachment is the presence of emotional pain when there is separation. When attached to someone, there is anxiety and even anger when we are separated from them. Like a baby with separation anxiety, we feel afraid, stressed, and may even feel angry when not near to those with whom we are attached.

5. Those with attachments experience loss and grief.

We don't really miss someone with whom we have no relationship, and we generally do not feel pain when separated from those we do not love. When there is a break in our attached relationships, there is a real sense of loss and grief, which is painful and depressing at deep heart levels. We miss them and have an ache deep inside that is longing to be present with them.

6. They have an enduring bond from the cradle to the grave.

An attachment is an enduring emotional bond that connects one person to another across time and space. An attachment by definition has the enduring quality of being without end.

7. There is a quality of caregiver/receiver dynamic.

A true attachment does not have to be two-sided but always has the quality of giving and receiving. This does not mean that we give and exchange evenly. As a parent often gives without receiving much back in return, so attachments can be one-sided at times. However, there is always an element of give and take, giving and receiving in attachment dynamics. The essential quality of true attachment is that their relational interactions take place in a natural flow of give and take that we call "Synchronization."

8. Attachments meet one's need for protection, safety, and comfort.

The Journey into the Divided Heart

We have a God-given need to feel protected, safe, and comforted by others. Attachments result in joy and contentment. Just like a baby with its parents, we gain a sense of protection, safety, and comfort within these intimate relationships, even as adults.

In attachment, then, there is accessibility to all the resources of the other because there is a constant sharing back and forth between the two living in sync! In attachment there is a never-ending bond that, like a baby to its mother, brings a security that is beyond anxiety and hopelessness. Attachment grants a secure base from which to explore the world, and like a toddler taking risks to venture outside of his or her comfort zone that secure base gives the strength and confidence necessary to fuel those steps forward. These factors, researched and found by John Bowlby, are a great way to describe the true loving relationship that the Father God offers us through His Son, Jesus. What great blessings come to us from true attachment in our relationships. They are worth the risk of hurt and emotional pain inherent in this level of intimacy!

The difficulty is that many of us, due to our life's circumstances, have never experienced the depth of blessing of a true attachment. Further, we have never learned to have the depth of relationship God intended. True attachment relationship is the glue of our minds and hearts that keeps our sanity and security in place. The heart without relationship is a heart with great depravity. The intervention needed here is simply to get our free will to choose to attach and reprogram the five levels of the brain to function together so we can gain attachment healing in intimacy with others! Although all the other interventions listed before this are crucial to our emotional healing, in some ways they all lead up to this one intervention. They free us up and equip us to take steps toward true relationship, which is the only place, according to the Scripture and attachment theory, that we will experience the love, joy, and peace that we were created to have.

Even in major league baseball, only the best players get a hit a third of the time. We will strike out, fail, get hit by the ball, and fall flat on our face, maybe even a majority of the time. But when we stop going up to the plate, that is when we really lose! When we stop pursuing the God-given needs we have for attachment, that is when we lose! Choosing to relate and attach is a risk, but it is the risk with the potential for the greatest payoff in our lives. Intimacy!

THE FIRST KEY TO TRUE RELATIONSHIP IS IN LEARNING HOW TO RECEIVE!

Did you ever consider that true relationship is not possible without being able to receive? Our very survival depends on receiving. How can a baby even survive unless she receives milk from her mother's breast? How can we breathe without receiving air, or eat without taking in food that God gives and provides? The danger and real damage that our defenses bring with them is that, though they appear to prevent some hurt in our lives, they are actually creating barriers that keep us from receiving every good thing that God and people have to give to us! A defensive stance is a preventative stance, and in trying to keep out all that is bad, our defenses are also keeping out all that is good. We have a good God who loves to give good gifts to His children (James 1:17). If we are blockaded behind our defense mechanisms, God will not break our free will to impose on us. Even the good things He has for us like His love, peace, joy, and healing must be received. God will not override our free will. The greatest gifts in this world are not materialistic in nature; they are divine and spiritual in nature. They are just waiting to be received!

When we choose to let our walls down and begin to receive, it is then that we can receive from our relationships the love that they have been trying to give us. Practice makes perfect. Over time we want to learn to be mindful of gifts that come in packages that we would not normally recognize. This is very important to our health and growth in knowing that all things received really came from God above (James 1:17). Is it hard for you to receive compliments and encouragements? Just being told that they did a good job or that they look nice can be difficult for many people. If they really track their thoughts, they will tell you that they feel resistance, an instant response of some sort that pushes away those compliments. Many reply, "Oh, it was nothing." Is that you? Do you redirect the discussion away from you when being complimented? Why do you think receiving is so hard for you? What would happen if you just said "thank you" and received those words as a sincere compliment? You probably just feel a little too vulnerable when being complimented, so you decide somewhere in your divided heart to push away all praise. How sad this scenario is for both parties—the receiver and those trying to give.

Receiving gets harder on deeper, more personal levels of vulnerability too. How do you do with receiving physical touch? This is a big one for many people. They have shared with me some of the internal chatter they hear as soon as someone looks like they are going to touch them. Lots of defenses go up for the wounded heart when others try to hug, kiss, or even just shake their hands. Though their divided heart looks for touch and craves it somewhere inside, they push it away.

How confusing for the divided heart and for those wanting to love us! Touch is a basic human need. Just like babies require touch to live and thrive from birth, we as adults have the same basic need whether we want to admit it or not. We defensively look at touch as being much too vulnerable, but our hearts tell us that we need affection like we need the air that we breathe. Touch is one of the best conflict resolution skills because it is hard to be angry while we are holding someone's hand. Touch is one of the best calming agents because when our fear and tension have us all worked up inside, a touch tells us that we are not alone and grounds us back to a secure and safe place of connectedness with someone else. Some psychiatrists believe that kids *need* touch at least a 100 times a day. How many touches do you need a day? Touch is a big part of attachment!

The Bible gives an amazing metaphor to help us understand attachment and how we all need each other in a give-and-take relationship under the headship of Christ.

> *"Just as a body, though one, has many parts, but all*
> *its many parts form one body, so it is with Christ. For*
> *we were all baptized by[a] one Spirit so as to form one*
> *body—whether Jews or Gentiles, slave or free—and we*

were all given the one Spirit to drink. Even so the body is not made up of one part but of many. Now if the foot should say, 'Because I am not a hand, I do not belong to the body,' it would not for that reason stop being part of the body" (1 Corinthians 12:12-15).

The parts cannot say to each other, "I do not need you," and the foot cannot say to the hand, "I can live life without you." That would be ridiculous. There is an attachment as close as the hand is to the finger that preserves the individuality of each part but recognizes that the finger and the hand separately have little effectiveness without putting them together. The hand and the fingers complement each other; they also highlight for each other what their true purpose and meaning is all about. As we attach to others, we can still preserve the unique and individual self-worth of who we are. At an even deeper level, we will experience a joyful revelation of who we truly are made to be by our Creator when we are functioning with the attachments He has planned for us.

The real danger of our defensiveness is that the attachments that God meant us to have are not able to operate within the confines of our own personal fortresses. Attaching requires a vulnerability and openness to others that is the opposite of being defensive. As we learn to receive from others, we will also learn to receive from God. He has so much to give to us! As we attach, we may go through the fire and get heated up as two metals are in the welding process. We may feel stuck, trapped, and insecure as we are united with others, but if we allow God to do it His way the process will bring out the best and worst of who we are. It will bring to the surface those defense mechanisms that are still left and that need to be thrown in the proverbial trash!

God made us to *need* real relationships, not just acquaintances. He has relationships lined up to bless us, but our defenses can keep that from happening. It is time to pray the following prayer and take responsibility for the loneliness that we feel deep down inside. We crave attachments because that is how God built us. It is our lonely emptiness that leads us to addictions as well as the growing anxiety and depression we are experiencing. Praying the following words is a beginning step. It works by using our free will to allow God to bring us the relationships to which He wants us to attach.

Dear Father God, I come to You today and acknowledge both my need for You and my need for other people in my life. I realize that I was created to need people as a foundation of my joy. Father God, I repent for any and all the defenses my divided heart has used to protect me, which have in themselves kept me from the attachments that my heart needs. I ask You to forgive me and to teach me how to live my life with You as my defender, my safe home base, and my security. I choose to allow my heart to attach to those You direct me to know and to learn to give and to receive from them in healthy and holy ways. I am humbled at my need for others and recognize that attachments are a blessing from You, God. I acknowledge that there will be emotional pain inherent to my decision to trust these attachments deeply, and I ask You for the grace to endure without detaching during these times. I take responsibility for my decisions that have led to my own lack of attachments, and I ask You to bring a depth of relationship into my life with You and with others that will allow me to experience Your true joy. Amen.

Chapter 30: Community Living

Now that you have taken a good look at your defense mechanisms, prayed through your decision to heal the deep places inside your heart and soul, looked at the interventions of repentance and salvation, learned to reframe and set good healthy boundaries, gotten inner healing, and learned some about fighting the spiritual battle inside of you, you are ready to attach, but not just on an individual level! Now it's time to go out and let that big, old, healed heart of yours become a part of something bigger. The heart unified and not divided will naturally be drawn to not only attach to one or two people but to a community of people where they can be part of something bigger.

The world is searching for true community; we were hardwired by our Creator to want and need it! People are subconsciously looking for true relational community everywhere they go. If they do not find it in their family, their churches, and their neighborhoods they will huddle up around any commonality to bring them together. People are looking in bars for community. They find parts of community there as there is a true feeling of togetherness in their experience, but it comes with a self-centered backdrop of lust and buzzed-up good times. They're looking for community on social media, trying to stay connected by staying up to date on the most finite of details in each other's lives, but without the emotional risk of true togetherness. They are looking for the elements of community in their common purposes at work because community does have at its heart purpose and progress. The essence of community can be found in the ways everyone uses their talents as a group to accomplish what the individual could not. Some use involvement in sports teams as their community; others are part of theater and singing groups and social clubs. Even human service organizations offer the elements of activity and service to others, which we desire. The church was created to be the truest form of community as it was made for all of the above reasons, but with a standard, a power, and a love that breeds life to its fullest (John 10:10). One body under one head directing them all, being Christ.

It's time to join a church! Join an imperfect church, as they all are, and don't just focus on its weaknesses. Become part of the solution! Bring all that we have been reading about to the table—model an undivided heart to those around you and attach with a zeal that will show the world the love of God. As the song says, "They will know we are Christians by our love" (see John 13:35)! Don't just go to make friends but to be a friend. Focus on the giving part of the attachment relationships you build, and the receiving will come if you will let it. Get under the trusted authority of some leaders in your life who have been places you have not. Submit yourself to them, trust them, and you will build your relational capacity as well as new levels of trust if you work at not being offended! As in twelve-step programs, the Christian leaders in your life can become like sponsors who will provide the accountability and loving discipline that will keep you headed in the right direction. Finding a band of brothers (or sisters) will provide for all the adventure your community-oriented heart desires as you fight each other's battles shoulder to shoulder and take ground in the world around you, making it better for all to enjoy.

Keep growing and learning, not only addressing your divided heart and the idols of your own self-protection, but taking risks to help others come to a single-mindedness to love and be loved. You can have the intimacy of knowing the details of each other's lives at a much deeper level than social media could ever give. You can have the common purpose of spreading love and good-will to your neighborhood, and you can do it all in safety with God as the middle, God as the standard, and God as the source of everything good—within the common union of relationships within the church!

Conclusion

I hope you have learned a lot, been challenged, and even healed to some extent as you have read and prayed through *The Jouney into the Divided Heart*. You have learned a lot about the process of healing emotionally, and you have understood that the spiritual aspect of emotional healing is the most neglected part. We need healing of all three parts—the body, the soul, *and* the spirit. You have been taken through seventeen defense mechanisms and learned that we have the choice to either give God the role as our protector or fill that job ourselves. You have read about nine interventions meant to help lead you to a unified, healed, and whole heart from which to live life to its fullest. Now you begin, or continue, to walk out the process of applying what you have learned to everyday life.

Be patient with yourself and with others as you do this. It takes time to reach the results that you desire. The healing of the heart is a process that starts with a single decision and a single prayer, but in reality it doesn't end until our days on earth are finished. Viewing healing as a lifelong process will protect you from discouragement and from the condemning judgments of yourself and others. You will see many victories and some failures along this road, but even the battles you lose have the potential to work for good. All life lessons are a protection for you. I used to think that healing was an event, and it is true that sometimes major victories are gained in one sitting, but it is more accurate to consider healing as a process. In fact, one of the main Greek words used in the Bible that is translated "healing" is *therapeuo*.[12] It is used in the Bible forty-three times and is used commonly as our English word *therapy*. Therapy is a healing in process; it is what you and your counselor, your pastor, and your inner circle of friends will be walking out as you apply what you have learned in this book. This doesn't mean you will need to be in therapy for your entire life. It just means you will learn these tools and the means to apply them and practice them with others whom you love until you reach perfection in heaven.

The healing process reminds me a lot of the process we went through when we were replacing the roof of the 150-year-old dairy farm that we were converting into a church. I still remember peeling the first layer of rubber off the flat roof, thinking maybe we would have to throw a few layers of shingles away that may be underneath. Our jaws dropped when we peeled back one layer, two, then three, and on and on it went. Some of the layers weren't just a thin line of shingles but a thicker, water-logged, mildewed, smelly, soggy layer of nastiness that was over a foot thick! Even after we peeled off all the old layers, we found that the original foundational layer was made of rotten and broken 2 x 6 boards. It wasn't easy work to keep us all from falling through! Working on that roof month after month brought many of us some great healing as we got to see our divided hearts exposed. We took on a project together for our community with gladness and excitement, but the hard, smelly work also made us want to run and hide from this ongoing backbreaking project that felt like it would never end.

God spoke to us and said that the condition of our hearts was like that roof, and that He was taking us through the same process internally that we were accomplishing externally. The layers of shingles symbolized the layers of calluses, scars, wounds, strongholds, and generations of dividedness from God that we had learned from our culture and the world around us. Layer after layer

---

12. Thayer and Smith, "Greek Lexicon entry for Therapeuo," The KJV New Testament Greek Lexicon, Accessed February 2, 2017, http://www.biblestudytools.com/lexicons/greek/kjv/therapeuo.html.

had been laid down as temporary fixes for the broken foundation underneath. It's like putting bandage after bandage on top of a deep, festering wound. The result was a deteriorating roof that leaked like a sieve. Likewise, the condition of our emotional hearts had deteriorated to the point that we all are not functioning as well as we could either. God has plans to renew our hearts down to their very foundations, just as we did our church roof.

The interventions listed in this book will lead you to do the same. Don't settle for putting another layer of shingles on your roof to temporarily hide the dysfunction beneath it; that is what many do in the church and in counseling today. I thank God for the discontent I have had in my spirit ever since being led into the field of counseling. As I related before, it wasn't long before I realized that the help I was bringing to people was only short-lived; their overall condition was often ending up worse in the end. I almost burned out and gave up as I worked and ministered at multiple places, occasionally finding pieces of what I knew was the path to healing along the way. But there was always something missing and the result was always far less than what I saw in the ministry of Jesus when I read the Bible.

Even when I found the tools I have listed above and the truths that were leading many people into what I considered to be miraculous healings of various traumas, deliverance from demonic strongholds, saved marriages, and people walking into new and more functional ways of thinking and relating to others, I still felt discouraged at times. I think I just thought that at some point the battles would come to an end for people. I kept waiting for us to get over the hump and coast downhill. But that's not how it works at all. It turns out that, like the Israelites when taking the Promised Land, there is always more ground to take. When we allow the Holy Spirit to do His work, there are always times of rest and healing, but they are followed by the next season of battles and hard steps needed to take more emotional ground. My clients and I have found greater peace when we realized we can live in the moment, no matter what it is, and hope for the future with blessed results. To live in the moment, one day at a time, seeing that the goal is not perfection as much as enjoying the process, regardless of the season we are in is a good way to live.

You will find, as I have and as my clients have, that victory does not necessarily look like you think it does, and that as the Bible says *"When I am weak, then I am strong"* (2 Corinthians 12:10). God gives grace to the humble but opposes the proud (James 4:6), and oftentimes His goal is to lead us to deeper humility so that we learn to lean on Him and not ourselves. What if that is what the undivided heart is all about? What if it is not about getting to the point where we are nothing but happy-happy joy-joy all the time, or performing well, never sinning, having perfect marriages and relationships without conflict? What if the goal is to know that we are to live in a constant state of needing Him and depending upon Him for our every breath, our very peace, and every move we make? That place of humility, of weakness, of not needing to be perfect or strong is the place where our hearts find contentment.

My journey, like yours, is a masterpiece of lessons learned. I thank God that He brought me to a place of knowing that I needed Him at an early age. I thank Him for my parents and family, loving pastors and teachers from an early age, godly friends from the time I was very young, and God's great mercy through the ups and downs of daily life, ministry, marriage, parenting, business, and community life. I can see after many years of practicing what I have described in *The Journey into the Divided Heart* that each new difficulty and trial in my life has served for my good and well-being. I can see better today than ever that there is a great God with a great plan that has been building my character and helping me with the division and turmoil of walking in my own divided heart. I can see how there is a devil that has thrown everything but the kitchen sink at me, my family, and those walking this same road (which is many of my readers, too, I am sure). I can see how I have made many mistakes—hindsight is 20/20 as they say—but I can also see the risks that I

Conclusion

took and the mistakes that I made have allowed me to grow into who I am. They allow me to do what I do effectively! I am realizing my calling and purpose. This is the ultimate goal for us all! My heart is less divided than ever before, but there is much more to be exposed by the day-to-day triggers of everyday life.

I believe that God has a plan for you! I believe that the trials you are experiencing are working for your good. I believe that you are loved though your heart is divided and that you are walking both with and against God's ways in your everyday life. You may be very close to realizing that you are loved by God, no matter how you react and perform. You may be very close to some major victories as you discover that most of the mistakes you make are rooted in the emotional pain stored in the foundation of your heart and mind. No one can be expected to not swear if they hit their thumb with a hammer, and your decision-making in reaction to your emotional pain when it is triggered is understandable too.

If there is one thing you learned through this book, I hope it is that you have a responsibility not to be perfect, but a responsibility to choose! And choose you will, after reading this book, the Scriptures, and the tools gathered from so many places of ministry and psychology; you now have choices to make. Your choice to do something or nothing has great consequences and rewards. As Joshua laid out the two paths of being blessed or cursed, following God's path or not, so I do for you today:

> *"But if serving the Lord seems undesirable to you, then choose for yourselves this day whom you will serve, whether the gods your forefathers served beyond the River, or the gods of the Amorites, in whose land you are living. But as for me and my household, we will serve the Lord"* (Joshua 24:15).

Though it seems you can be a Gomer and follow two loves at the same time, God's message was really very simple. Following two paths is not following His path at all. Doing nothing with what you

243

have learned is still doing something. Not making a choice is making a choice. Your next step in counseling, in therapy, in meeting with your pastor, in talking with your spouse and family and friends is to choose this day whom you will serve.

I didn't know that when the majority of this book flowed out of me almost seven years ago and when I put it on the shelf, waiting for direction from Him, that His timing would be as perfect as it was. I did not know that I would have the great privilege to have a thriving Christian counseling practice, seeing hundreds of people a week in our facilities, and that there would be thousands if not ten thousands who had received ministry through Renewal Christian Counseling Center. I am thankful for every client; we have learned these tools together! And now I am thankful for each reader of this book who will also learn and grow with all of us together.

When sitting on my boat, minding my own business this past summer, I heard the voice of my Savior loud and clear: "I am not done with that book you wrote many years ago." I could not deny that it was Him, and I can see now that I was not just sharing principles as I wrote. I was sharing a lifestyle that I have learned to walk in much more consistently than I was when I first began to write. He said to me, "The divided heart is a call to repentance." What you just read is more than a counseling manual or a self-help treatise on emotional healing. It is a call to God's people to a deeper place of repentance, past their actions and behaviors to a place where they can take a practical inventory that will expose the motives of the heart (1 Corinthians 4:5).

Won't you choose to repent of all the ways you try to be your own protector and give Him that job today? He is fitted for it, and you can trust Him to care for you well. I would love to hear from you and walk out this call of repentance with you. I can connect you to resources and others who have begun the process of addressing their divided hearts. You may contact me at **steve@dividedheart.org** and share the testimony of what God did in your heart as you have read these pages, ask for a counselor at Renewal Center, ask your questions, or link with

Conclusion

our ministry as a resource to others who are making decisions toward change.

May God's grace and love rest on your journey! Amen.

Ministries Referenced

- American Association of Christian Counseling: aacc.net
- Cloud Townsend Resources (Boundaries Books): cloudtownsend.com
- HeartSynch Ministries, Father Andrew Miller: heartsynchministries.org
- Immanuel Approach: immanuelapproach.com
- Renewal Christian Counseling Center: renewalcenter.org
- Restoration in Christ: rcm-usa.org
- Shepherd's House: joystartshere.com
- Sozo: bethelsozo.com
- Transformation Prayer Ministries: transformationprayer.org

Addendum

This test[13] was taken from counselingresource.com, a site that has this and many other helpful resources. Take a minute with this simple test and be honest with yourself, looking inside to see to what extent you experience dissociation.

The Dissociative Experiences Scale (DES), A Screening Test for Dissociative Identity Disorder

This twenty-eight question self-test has been developed as a screening test for Dissociative Identity Disorder, formerly known as Multiple Personality Disorder. This questionnaire consists of twenty-eight questions about experiences that you may have had in your daily life. We are interested in how often you have these experiences. It is important, however, that your answers show how often these experiences happen to you when you are not under the influence of alcohol or drugs.

To answer the questions, please determine to what degree the experience described in the question applies to you and choose the button which corresponds to the percentage of the time you have the experience. The left of the scale, labeled "Never," corresponds to 0 percent of the time, while the right of the scale, labeled "Always,"

---

13. Staff, CounsellingResource Research. "Dissociative Experiences Scale." CounsellingResource.com: Psychology, Therapy & Mental Health Resources. 2011. Accessed December 01, 2016. http://counsellingresource.com/quizzes/misc-tests/des.

corresponds to 100 percent of the time; the range covers 0 percent to 100 percent in 10 percent increments.

Take the Quiz

Please note: This test will only be scored correctly if you answer each one of the questions.

1. Some people have the experience of driving or riding in a car or bus or subway and suddenly realizing that they don't remember what has happened during all or part of the trip.

(Never) ☐ ☐ ☐ ☐ ☐ ☐ ☐ ☐ ☐ ☐ ☐ (Always)

2. Some people find that sometimes they are listening to someone talk and they suddenly realize that they did not hear part or all of what was said.

(Never) ☐ ☐ ☐ ☐ ☐ ☐ ☐ ☐ ☐ ☐ ☐ (Always)

3. Some people have the experience of finding themselves in a place and having no idea how they got there.

(Never) ☐ ☐ ☐ ☐ ☐ ☐ ☐ ☐ ☐ ☐ ☐ (Always)

4. Some people have the experience of finding themselves dressed in clothes that they don't remember putting on.

(Never) ☐ ☐ ☐ ☐ ☐ ☐ ☐ ☐ ☐ ☐ ☐ (Always)

5. Some people have the experience of finding new things among their belongings that they do not remember buying.

(Never) ☐ ☐ ☐ ☐ ☐ ☐ ☐ ☐ ☐ ☐ ☐ (Always)

6. Some people sometimes find that they are approached by people they do not know who call them by another name or insist that they have met them before.

(Never) ☐ ☐ ☐ ☐ ☐ ☐ ☐ ☐ ☐ ☐ ☐ (Always)

7. Some people sometimes have the experience of feeling as though they are standing next to themselves or watching themselves do something and they actually see themselves as if they were looking at another person.

(Never) ☐ ☐ ☐ ☐ ☐ ☐ ☐ ☐ ☐ ☐ ☐ (Always)

8. Some people are told that they sometimes do not recognize friends or family members.

(Never) ☐ ☐ ☐ ☐ ☐ ☐ ☐ ☐ ☐ ☐ ☐ (Always)

9. Some people find that they have no memory for some important events in their lives (for example, a wedding or graduation).

(Never) ☐ ☐ ☐ ☐ ☐ ☐ ☐ ☐ ☐ ☐ ☐ (Always)

10. Some people have the experience of being accused of lying when they do not think that they have lied.

(Never) ☐ ☐ ☐ ☐ ☐ ☐ ☐ ☐ ☐ ☐ ☐ (Always)

11. Some people have the experience of looking in a mirror and not recognizing themselves.

(Never) ☐ ☐ ☐ ☐ ☐ ☐ ☐ ☐ ☐ ☐ ☐ (Always)

12. Some people have the experience of feeling that other people, objects, and the world around them are not real.

(Never) ☐ ☐ ☐ ☐ ☐ ☐ ☐ ☐ ☐ ☐ ☐ (Always)

13. Some people have the experience of feeling that their body does not seem to belong to them.

(Never) ☐ ☐ ☐ ☐ ☐ ☐ ☐ ☐ ☐ ☐ ☐ (Always)

14. Some people have the experience of sometimes remembering a past event so vividly that they feel as if they were reliving that event.

(Never) ☐ ☐ ☐ ☐ ☐ ☐ ☐ ☐ ☐ ☐ ☐ (Always)

15. Some people have the experience of not being sure whether things that they remember happening really did happen or whether they just dreamed them.

(Never) ☐ ☐ ☐ ☐ ☐ ☐ ☐ ☐ ☐ ☐ ☐ (Always)

16. Some people have the experience of being in a familiar place but finding it strange and unfamiliar.

(Never) ☐ ☐ ☐ ☐ ☐ ☐ ☐ ☐ ☐ ☐ ☐ (Always)

17. Some people find that when they are watching television or a movie they become so absorbed in the story that they are unaware of other events happening around them.

(Never) ☐ ☐ ☐ ☐ ☐ ☐ ☐ ☐ ☐ ☐ ☐ (Always)

18. Some people find that they become so involved in a fantasy or daydream that it feels as though it were really happening to them.

(Never) ☐ ☐ ☐ ☐ ☐ ☐ ☐ ☐ ☐ ☐ ☐ (Always)

19. Some people find that they sometimes are able to ignore pain.

(Never) ☐ ☐ ☐ ☐ ☐ ☐ ☐ ☐ ☐ ☐ ☐ (Always)

20. Some people find that they sometimes sit staring off into space, thinking of nothing, and are not aware of the passage of time.

(Never) ⬚ ⬚ ⬚ ⬚ ⬚ ⬚ ⬚ ⬚ ⬚ ⬚ ⬚ (Always)

21. Some people sometimes find that when they are alone they talk out loud to themselves.

(Never) ⬚ ⬚ ⬚ ⬚ ⬚ ⬚ ⬚ ⬚ ⬚ ⬚ ⬚ (Always)

22. Some people find that in one situation they may act so differently compared with another situation that they feel almost as if they were two different people.

(Never) ⬚ ⬚ ⬚ ⬚ ⬚ ⬚ ⬚ ⬚ ⬚ ⬚ ⬚ (Always)

23. Some people sometimes find that in certain situations they are able to do things with amazing ease and spontaneity that would usually be difficult for them (for example, sports, work, social situations, etc.).

(Never) ⬚ ⬚ ⬚ ⬚ ⬚ ⬚ ⬚ ⬚ ⬚ ⬚ ⬚ (Always)

24. Some people sometimes find that they cannot remember whether they have done something or have just thought about doing it (for example, not knowing whether they have just mailed a letter or have just thought about mailing it).

(Never) ⬚ ⬚ ⬚ ⬚ ⬚ ⬚ ⬚ ⬚ ⬚ ⬚ ⬚ (Always)

25. Some people find evidence that they have done things that they do not remember doing.

(Never) ⬚ ⬚ ⬚ ⬚ ⬚ ⬚ ⬚ ⬚ ⬚ ⬚ ⬚ (Always)

26. Some people sometimes find writings, drawings, or notes among their belongings that they must have done but cannot remember doing.
(Never) ▯ ▯ ▯ ▯ ▯ ▯ ▯ ▯ ▯ ▯ ▯ (Always)

27. Some people sometimes find that they hear voices inside their head that tell them to do things or comment on things that they are doing.
(Never) ▯ ▯ ▯ ▯ ▯ ▯ ▯ ▯ ▯ ▯ ▯ (Always)

28. Some people sometimes feel as if they are looking at the world through a fog so that people and objects appear far away or unclear.
(Never) ▯ ▯ ▯ ▯ ▯ ▯ ▯ ▯ ▯ ▯ ▯ (Always)

This screening test for Dissociative Identity Disorder is scored by totaling the percentage answered for each question (from 0 percent to 100 percent) and then dividing by 28—this yields a score in the range of 0 to 100.

Generally speaking, the higher the DES score, the more likely it is that the person has DID. In a sample of 1,051 clinical subjects, however, only 17 percent of those scoring above 30 on the DES actually had DID.

The DES is not a diagnostic instrument. It is a screening instrument. High scores on the DES do not prove that a person has a dissociative disorder; they only suggest that clinical assessment for dissociation is warranted. People experiencing DID do sometimes have low scores, so a low score does not rule out DID. In fact, given that in most studies the average DES score for a DID person is in the 40s, with a standard deviation of about 20, roughly 15 percent of clinically diagnosed DID patients score below 20 on the DES.

Always consult with a trained mental health professional if you are experiencing depressive feelings and/or difficulties in your daily functioning that cause you anxiety or worry. **This test is meant to be used as a starting point, not as a diagnosis tool. This score is not intended as a mental disorder diagnosis or as any type of healthcare recommendation.**

About the Author

Steve Fair is the founder and the director of Renewal Christian Counseling Center which was started in 2001 and was birthed out of his desire to see a new depth and power in the counseling field come through providing cutting edge clinical, medical, and spiritual interventions to those whose hearts are hurting and broken. He has his ministry degree from MorningStar Ministries in Fort Mill, SC, and has ministered as a speaker, teacher, and counselor for the last twenty-five years in Michigan. He received his master's degree in social work from the University of Michigan in 1995. Steve and his wife, Mindy, have been married for twenty-two years and have one son, Ryan.

Steve can be contacted at steve@dividedheartbook.com.